Understanding Alcohol and Drug Addiction

AN LDS PERSPECTIVE

BY

MERLIN O. BAKER

UNDERSTANDING ALCOHOL AND DRUG ADDICTION

AN LDS PERSPECTIVE

BY

MERLIN O. BAKER

ISBN: 1-55517-777-8
e. 1

Published by CFI
an imprint of Cedar Fort Inc.
www.cedarfort.com

Distributed by:

Cover design by Nicole Shaffer
Cover design © 2004 by Lyle Mortimer

Printed in the United States of America
10 9 8 7 6 5 4 3 2 1

Printed on acid-free paper

Merlin Baker identifies the spiritual pathway that brings the gospel into addiction treatment—replacing *I am powerless* with *I have the power of God.* The book is organized to help each person and family plagued with addictions to find and use this spiritual pathway.

—Dr. Edwin Brown, PhD, LCSW, LMRT
    Clinical Director: Renaissance Ranch Adult Addiction
    Treatment Center

Jeffrey R. Holland of the Quorum of the Twelve calls the Church "*not* a monastery for the holy, but a hospital for the sick." LDS Church members are just awakening to the awful realities of the disease of chemical addiction that ravages many of its members; addiction can strike anyone.

Rescuing the lost sheep through our Savior and Redeemer Jesus Christ includes rescuing those who have fallen into the mire of chemical addiction. Merlin Baker has a personal connection to this rescue operation, both as a parent of an addicted child and as a missionary working directly with the LDS addiction recovery program. He has written a sensitive, very readable, and helpful discourse on the disease of addiction—and what we, as loved ones and "fellow citizens in the household of faith" can do to help those entrapped by this disease and to guard against it. I recommend this book for all LDS leaders and families.

—Stephen G. Biddulph, MA, LPC/LSAC
    Author: *Hazelden Adolescent Recovery Plan* and *What's a Parent to Believe*
    Alcohol Director: Red Rock Canyon School for Adolescence Recovery

I dedicate this book to my wife Marian,
and all those missionaries who love and labor
in the service of those who struggle with addictions.

TO THOSE WHO SUFFER

I would rescue you, if I could,
But you are beyond the reach of my desire.

I would bear your pain,
If somehow your pain could be mine,

But I must wait with outstretched arms,
Of love and hope and prayer,

'Til the enemy has been subdued,
And you with Christ have conquered all.

Contents

Preface

As I have served as a missionary in the LDS Addiction Recovery Program, two realities continue to be impressed upon my heart and mind: first, the incalculable pain and despair that the addict and his family endure because of the curse of alcohol and drug addiction; and second, the lack of knowledge and understanding by the members and leaders of the Church about alcohol and drug addiction, treatment, and recovery.

I hope that this book will help addicts and their families as well as members and leaders of the Church in understanding alcohol and drug addiction, treatment, and recovery—and help replace anguish and despair with hope, recovery, and joy.

I am grateful for the support and encouragement of my sweet wife, Marian, in writing this book, as well as her help in processing draft after draft. I'm grateful to my daughters, Michelle and Shannon for their review and editorial suggestions in the final preparation of the manuscript and to my son Jonathan for his suggested changes. I want to thank three good friends, H.R. Brown, Steven Brown, and Kris Groves who reviewed the manuscript. And I'm thankful to those dear friends who consented to having their personal stories included in this book. Some of the stories in the book are derived from media sources and court records. In these instances the real names of the individuals involved have not been used.

The statements and opinions in this book are based solely upon the research and personal observations and experiences of the author, and they are not approved or endorsed by The Church of Jesus Christ of Latter-day Saints.

Introduction

According to Joseph A. Califano, Jr., former United States Secretary of Health, Education and Welfare and former President of the Center on Addiction and Substance Abuse, Columbia University, "Drug and alcohol abuse is America's number one health problem, the number one crime problem, the number one homeless problem, the number one youth problem, including youth violence."[1]

The devastation of alcoholism and drug addiction impacts the lives of millions of Americans each day. The destruction addiction causes cross over every social and economic line; no group is immune. Alcoholism and drug addiction are prevalent among rich and poor, educated and uneducated, young and old, male and female, as well as every racial, ethnic, and religious group.

In 2001, 16.6 million Americans age 12 or older were classified with dependence on or abuse of alcohol and drugs, a figure significantly higher than the 2000 figure of 14.5 million. The nationwide percentage rate in 2001 translates to about 7.3% of the U.S. population.[2] Approximately one-fourth of the U.S. population is part of a family affected by an addictive disorder in a first degree relative, and almost 90% of addicted individuals live with a family member or significant other.[3]

In Utah about 5% of adults and 7% of youth are in need of substance abuse treatment, a total of 89,701 individuals. The public substance abuse treatment system in Utah currently serves 22,836 individuals, or only 25% of the actual need.[4]

Roughly 100,000 Utahns, or one out of every 20, suffer from an addiction to alcohol or drugs. One-fifth of addicts are children under the age of 18. The average Utah addict is 31 years old, white and LDS. Two out of three are men. But women are fast catching up. The number of women admitted to addiction treatment centers increased by 144% the past year, compared to a 20% increase for men.[5]

The number of deaths from illegal drugs in Utah increased sixfold in the 1990s, from 20 in 1991 to 130 in 1998.[6] In Utah 60-70% of child abuse cases involve alcohol or drug abuse in the home.[7]

Many members of The Church of Jesus Christ of Latter-day Saints are alcoholics or drug addicts. Although most members of the Church are shielded from the addictive power of alcohol and drugs by their observance of the Word of Wisdom, many make wrong decisions and become caught in the terrible web and nightmare of addiction.

As indicated above, about 5% of Utah adults and 7.3% of persons over twelve in the U.S. are in need of substance abuse treatment. The percentage of Church members who are in need of substance abuse treatment is not available. However, hypothetically, a 3% figure and a ward population of 400 would compute to 12 members of a ward who need substance abuse treatment. Surrounding each substance abuser are three or four family members severely impacted by the addict's destructive behavior. Many family members impacted by the addiction of a loved one are in denial and do not want the bishop or ward members to know of their problem. The social stigma they feel is very powerful.

The scourge of alcoholism and drug addiction may never be lifted from the human family, but effective prevention and treatment can lessen its toll of human tragedy and suffering. Understanding alcohol and drug addiction, the available treatment, and the process of recovery is central to effective prevention and treatment.

The purpose of this book is to present basic information about alcohol and drug addiction, treatment and recovery. Any member of the Church who has lived with an addicted family member can testify that it is a living hell. Hopefully, the material in this book will help addicts and their families find the road to recovery. Alcohol and drug addiction and treatment are complex and multi-faceted problems. Professional help should be sought by addicts and their families in making decisions regarding intervention and treatment options.

Chapter 10 includes personal stories of individuals who have been successful in putting their disease of addiction into remission, allowing them to live quality lives and enjoy all of the blessings of the gospel. Appendix A is a suggested reading list. Appendix B is a list of organizations that offer materials on addiction, treatment, recovery, and prevention.

1

Alcohol and Drug Addiction—
Disease or Moral Failure?

Are alcohol and drug addiction diseases, or are they moral failure or a lack of will power on the part of the addict? The debate over this question has been going on for generations and continues today. The answer is that both are correct. Individuals who choose to drink or use drugs do so because it makes them feel better, happier, less depressed or less anxious. Alcoholics are frequently heard to say, "I loved to drink." The drug addict loves the "intense high" produced by the drug.

Alcohol and drugs cause a series of temporary changes in the brain that produce a "high," a rush of euphoria. People know that alcohol and drugs have the potential for addiction when they start using; however, they may think that they will not become addicted and that they can stop at any time. Most junior high and high schools have drug and alcohol prevention courses where the dangers of addiction are discussed. Addicts cannot really say they were never advised or did not know of the addictive potential of alcohol or drugs.

Furthermore, no one who is a member of The Church of Jesus Christ of Latter-day Saints can say that he or she was not warned about the evils and dangers of drinking or using drugs. The Word of Wisdom is a basic tenet of the Church. Adherence to the Word of Wisdom is a requirement for baptism, having a temple recommend, and holding an office in the Church. The promises of the Word of Wisdom are both temporal and spiritual. Those who keep this commandment shall have "health in their navel and marrow to their bones, And shall find wisdom and great treasures of knowledge, even hidden treasures; And shall run and not be weary, and shall walk and not faint" (D&C 89:18-20).

President Gordon B. Hinckley has said:

> Be smart. Do not be so shortsighted as to indulge in the use of alcohol, tobacco, and drugs. It simply is not smart to do so. It is stupid, if you will pardon that harsh word, to use cocaine, marijuana, or any of the other drugs that rob you of control of your mind. After every drug-induced "high," there is a reactionary "low."[1]

The LDS Church recognizes the continuing problem of alcoholism and drug abuse:

> Drug, alcohol, and other substance abuse continues to plague all of mankind. Its effects can devastate individuals, families, communities, and nations. The Church continues to be concerned with the improper and harmful use of drugs or similar substances under circumstances which would result in addiction, physical or mental impairment, or in lowering moral standards. Prevention, recognition, and treatment are essential elements in dealing with substance abuse problems. Substance abuse recovery groups supervised by local LDS Family Services agencies are available in some areas. Recovery and healing are ultimately available to all through the Atonement of Jesus Christ.[2]

The use of alcohol and drugs starts out to be fun. It produces a high, euphoria, and pleasure. However, continued use can turn into addiction which is a living hell. Individuals who use and then abuse alcohol and drugs have made morally wrong decisions. They willfully violate a commandment of God with full knowledge that they may become addicted. They voluntarily start down a road that leads to bondage and terrible suffering. They pay a terrible price for their disobedience.

Some individuals can drink or experiment with alcohol and actually abuse drugs without becoming addicted. The fact that some individuals who abuse drugs and alcohol over long periods of time do not become addicted reinforces in the mind of many that alcoholism and drug addiction are a lack of will power or a moral failure. Non-alcoholics look at alcoholics from their own perspective and experience— that of people who can control their drinking. The remark is often made, "If others can quit, why can't you?"

However, alcoholics and drug addicts have lost control. They now have such compelling urges to use that they will continue to drink or abuse drugs even in the face of massive negative consequences. Very frequently an alcoholic or drug addict, after going through an extensive rehabilitation program or hovering near death in an emergency room, will go out and use the very day of their release.

Many people continue to think of addiction as primarily a moral or character problem, something caused by degeneracy or lack of willpower. The attitude of many is summed up by the following quotation:

> Most of us have grown up valuing self-control, sober judgment, and self-reliance. We look at addiction as a disgrace—something to be ashamed of. Addiction represents lack of character and moral failure to us, and we look at addicts as people who are untrustworthy, unreliable, irresponsible, and self-centered. Many religions

view alcoholism and drug addiction as sinful. Ridding yourself of addiction, according to this line of thinking, involves realizing that you have a problem, repenting, and moving on in your life with renewed self-determination and responsibility.[3]

Any person who has had a family member who is an alcoholic or drug addict can testify that addiction is something more, a lot more, than a lack of willpower. Addicts truly have lost control. They have lost their agency. Addicts can sometimes stop drinking or using drugs for short periods of time. However, for the addict staying clean and sober is the challenge. Avoiding relapse is the goal. Addicts can "white knuckle" it for a short period of time, but being clean and sober over any extended period of time eludes them.

With respect to alcoholism, the American Medical Association stated in 1972:

Alcoholism is a primary, chronic disease with genetic, psychosocial, and environmental factors influencing its development and manifestations. The disease is often progressive and fatal. It is characterized by impaired control over drinking, preoccupation with the drug alcohol, use of alcohol despite adverse consequences, and distortions in thinking, most notably denial.[4]

The Church of Jesus Christ of Latter-day Saints in its resource manual for helping families with alcohol problems defines alcoholism as follows:

Alcoholism is a chronic disease, or disorder of behavior, characterized by the repeated drinking of alcoholic beverages to an extent that exceeds customary dietary use or ordinary compliance with the social drinking customs of the community, and that interferes with the drinker's health, interpersonal relations, or economic functioning.[5]

GENETIC AND ENVIRONMENTAL FACTORS OF ADDICTION

There is strong evidence that much vulnerability to alcohol is inherited. Alcoholics frequently have alcoholic fathers, mothers, grandparents, siblings, and children.

Genetics researchers are engaged in identifying the genes that confer this vulnerability and in developing ways to apply this information to clinical populations. The task is difficult because alcoholism is considered to be a polygenic disorder that is related to many different genes, each of which contributes only a portion of the vulnerability. The search for the relevant genes is being pursued in several settings.[6]

Many individuals use alcohol or drugs to self-medicate underlying psychiatric or mental illness such as depression, bi-polar disorder, anxiety disorder, schizophrenia, attention deficit hyperactivity (ADHD), and anti-social or borderline personality. Those who do not have a genetic predisposition to alcohol abuse or the foregoing psychiatric or mental illnesses that can lead to addiction should gratefully and meekly bow their heads and say, "Thank you, Heavenly Father" and repeat in their minds, "There but for the grace of God go I."

The socioeconomic class and environment that a person grows up in also contribute significantly to alcohol and drug addiction. Certainly, drug use by parents and older siblings and permissive parental attitudes toward drug use place all other children at great risk of drug use.

There is evidence that children who grow up in disorganized neighborhoods with high population density, high residential mobility, physical deterioration, and low levels of neighborhood attachment or cohesion, face greater risks for drug trafficking and drug abuse.[7]

Other factors that place children at greater risk of alcohol or drug use are: high levels of family conflict, lack of commitment to education by parents and children, and permissive or extremely authoritative parenting.[8]

ALCOHOL AND DRUG ADDICTION
AS A BRAIN DISEASE

There is ongoing medical evidence that addiction is actually a brain disease. Alan I. Lesher, Director of the National Institute on Drug Abuse, states:

> We now know that drug abuse is essentially a brain disease and should be addressed as such. It is not just a social problem or a moral failing on the part of addicts. It is important to state at the onset, however, that an individual's life decisions do play major roles both in the initial choice to use drugs and during the recovery process. . . . The more common view is that drug addicts are weak or bad people, unwilling to lead moral lives and to control their behavior and gratification.
>
> . . . The fact that addiction is tied to changes in brain structure and function is what makes it, fundamentally, a brain disease. Initially, drug use is voluntary, but prolonged use seems to throw a metaphorical 'switch' in the brain. Once that switch is thrown, the individual moves into the state of addiction characterized by compulsive drug seeking and use, even in the face of negative health and social consequences.[9]

Although the victim of a heart attack or stroke could be said to bring the disease on him or herself through diet and other lifestyle behaviors, once diagnosed, the disease is treated—not its long-distant origins. In this more productive concept, it makes little difference whether a disease is brought on by excessive exposure to fat or to abused drugs; one changes the functioning of the arteries and the heart, the other changes the functioning of the brain. Both require treatment.[10]

An addict's belief that his or her addiction is the result of moral failure or a lack of willpower can often delay treatment. Mistakenly, the addict believes that by exercising enough willpower he or she can overcome his addiction only to fail time and time again. Failure, guilt and shame make recovery even more difficult:

> One would think that guilt would enable recovery. Quite the opposite is true. Guilt, including but not limited to guilt about the addiction and the behaviors the patient engages to support his or her addiction, can seem so overwhelming that the only possible course is to obliterate the guilt through more substance abuse. The same is true for shame. The disease concept gives one a new attribution: "It wasn't me, it was my disease." This reduces guilt and shame and lessens the need to anesthetize one's mind to wipe out the guilt and the shame.[11]

Although addiction to alcohol and drugs is a disease of the brain, this does not excuse the addict from bearing the consequences of his or her destructive behavior. The addict started the chain of events that led to his or her addiction. Because of this, he or she should be held morally and legally responsible for all of the harm that his or her addiction caused to others. If an alcoholic is arrested for driving under the influence of alcohol, or injures or kills someone, he or she should be punished to the fullest extent of the criminal law. Drug addicts who steal and assault others to get money to support their habit should also be punished according to the criminal law. However, treatment should be made available to those who are in the jail and prison system.

Tougher laws for driving under the influence of alcohol

should be enacted. The legal limit for blood alcohol in many states is 0.08%. However, driving impairment occurs at a much lower percentage of blood alcohol. The United States Department of Transportation has set 0.02% as the maximum blood alcohol level for commercial drivers. No alcohol use before driving is the universal standard in Europe.[12]

Although addiction to alcohol or drugs is considered a disease, the alcoholic and the drug addict have a moral responsibility to seek treatment. Lesher states:

> Moreover, all addicts can and must participate in and take some significant responsibility for their own recovery. This brain disease does not erase self-control, but it does significantly erode one's ability to exert control over his or her behavior. This helps explain why an addict cannot simply stop using drugs by sheer force of will alone and must have treatment.[13]

It is important for the general public and members of the Church to understand and accept the disease concept of alcohol and drug addiction if treatment and recovery are to be understood and proper treatment decisions are to be made by the addict and his family. Addiction is a chronic and progressive disease. If not treated, addiction results in death. Treatment is multifaceted and long, even a life long process, where relapse, even many relapses are common. The addict and the family must never give up.

Acceptance of the disease concept of addiction does not diminish the moral and spiritual importance of the Word of Wisdom as a commandment of God or the reality of the spiritual and physical blessings that flow to individuals who obey it. How those who suffer the spiritual darkness and physical suffering of addiction wish that they had been obedient to its simple commands. There is great safety in obedience.

2
The Addictive Drugs
and the Pathway to Addiction

This chapter discusses the addictive drugs most widely used and the typical pathway to alcohol and drug addiction:

Alcohol
Marijuana
Cocaine
Heroin
Methamphetamine
Ecstacy
Prescription drugs

ALCOHOL

Alcohol is a drug, the most widely used of all the addictive drugs and the number one drug of abuse. Alcohol is a legal drug found in beer, wine, and distilled spirits. The difference among these beverages is in the concentration of alcohol. Alcohol and marijuana are sometimes called gateway drugs because their use provides a gateway to the use of cocaine, heroin, methamphetamines, and other synthetic drugs.[1]

Because alcohol is quickly and completely absorbed by the stomach directly into the bloodstream it influences the brain function almost immediately after ingestion. Alcohol is a depressant. It first affects the higher functions of the brain, including self control. The drinker first feels relaxed and uninhibited, sometimes saying and doing things that later they find embarrassing. Even small doses of alcohol can release the emotions of irritability and anger. In higher amounts, alcohol can produce lack of coordination, resulting in staggering and falling, and digestive upsets, particularly vomiting. Even larger doses can cause blackouts—where the intoxicated addict looks more or less normal, although intoxicated, but has no memory of what happened during the blackout.

Long-term use of alcohol leads to liver and brain damage. Alcohol use is also highly correlated with the use of other drugs and smoking. This multiplies the risk of cancer. Chronic alcohol use is a significant contributor to cancer of the mouth, esophagus, stomach, larynx, and lungs.

Excessive drinking is also a major cause of acute and chronic inflammation of the pancreas. Acute pancreatitis is one of the most painful of all diseases, producing an unrelenting knifelike pain in the middle abdomen that radiates to the back. This is an acute, recurring disease that can be fatal.

SHANE'S STORY. Shane was 21. He had been drinking and smoking since he was 15. Shane and his friend, John, took his dad's pickup truck and left from Salt Lake City to go camping with some friends. Shane and John had a few beers before they started. They stopped for gas along the way and picked up another 12-pack of beer. They continued to drink. As Shane was driving his right wheel hit the soft shoulder and flipped the truck over; it rolled three times. Shane had his seat belt on. John did not and was thrown from the truck. He was life-flighted to Salt Lake City. He is now in a coma and paralyzed from the neck down. Shane was arrested and charged with a DUI, the third one in two years. Shane wonders if John will survive and whether he will ever have the use of any of his limbs.

MARIJUANA

Marijuana, or pot, is a "gateway" drug that can lead to cocaine, meth and heroin use. Marijuana is usually smoked, although it can be swallowed. Marijuana is not injected or snorted as are cocaine and heroin.

The major cause of the high from marijuana is the chemical delta-9-tetrahydrocannabinol (THC) which is found in marijuana in concentrations of 1% to 5%. Marijuana contains more tar and cancer-causing chemicals than cigarette smoke. In fact, one marijuana cigarette has as much cancer causing tar as seventeen tobacco cigarettes. But marijuana's biggest effects are on a user's brain:

> The most striking effects of marijuana are on the user's brain. With occasional use, marijuana produces sedation and slightly altered mental processes. Learning is slowed, and concentration and short-term memory are hampered. Reaction times are slower and perceptions of time and distance are distorted, making driving and other safety-related behaviors especially hazardous after marijuana use. Users are commonly unaware of their impairments after using small doses of marijuana. Larger doses can precipitate acute anxiety or panic, or schizophrenic episodes, particularly for novice marijuana users and for people subject to these mental health disorders.

> . . . Marijuana makes users stupid and lazy. It is a careless drug, because pot users often lose the capacity to care. In the most extreme form, this is called the amotivational syndrome, meaning that chronic pot smokers become listless and apathetic, not just when using the drug but all of the time. This tragic state is called *burnout* by drug abusers themselves. Unlike cocaine, which often quickly brings users to their knees, marijuana claims its victims in a slower and more cruel fashion.

It robs many of them of their desire to grow and improve, often making heavy users settle for what is left over in life. For this reason, marijuana is the most insidious drug. Its effects are both profound and subtle.[2]

Marijuana users lose their purpose, will, memory, and motivation. Their performance sinks lower and lower and their hopes and lives literally go up in marijuana smoke.

COCAINE

Cocaine is derived from coca leaves grown in the Andes mountains in South America. Cocaine is a powerful stimulant and is available to drug abusers in two forms: a white, snow like powder, which is snorted or injected; and crack cocaine, small pellets or "rocks" that are smoked. When cocaine is snorted, the drug enters the bloodstream through the nasal membranes. Cocaine can also be injected in small amounts subcutaneously. This is known as skin popping because a small bubble forms just under the skin which disappears as the drug is absorbed.

Crack cocaine was introduced into the United States in the 1980's. Crack cocaine is made by mixing powdered cocaine with baking soda and water. Once the water evaporates, the mixture turns into a crystalline chunk or "rock" that is heated in a pipe and smoked. When the vapor is inhaled, the drug rushes to the brain producing a tremendous high or rush. A user of powder cocaine can spend several hundred dollars at a time, whereas crack cocaine, which is sold in small units, costs only five or ten dollars. Crack cocaine is now the dominant form of cocaine used.

Smoked crack cocaine hits the user's brain at very high levels within eight seconds, by far the fastest and most powerful way to get a drug high. Even intravenous use takes twice as long, or about sixteen seconds, to reach the brain. Peak effects occur within fifteen minutes of using cocaine by smoking or injecting and within thirty minutes by snorting the drug. The high of the cocaine is gone within an hour, although impairment of thinking can last for days or even weeks after high-dose use of cocaine.[3]

Cocaine use produces euphoria, an exaggerated sense of well-being and heightened energy. The user feels as if he or she can perform unusual acts of strength and intellectual performance. There is a loss of appetite and sleep becomes impossible for several hours after use.

The effects from a single use of cocaine last less than an hour, so cocaine users typically take the drug in 'runs,' meaning, they take repeated doses of cocaine every few minutes over periods of hours or days. The longer a cocaine run lasts, the less pleasure the cocaine user experiences with each use of the drug.

. . . Cocaine users usually feel depressed and exhausted at the end of a run of cocaine use, an experience called the "coke blues." Cocaine users not only feel terrible after a run of cocaine use, but they find they are unable to experience life's normal pleasures.[4]

Because the euphoric effect of cocaine use is of short duration, it encourages the user to keep using on a regular basis. Tolerance develops rapidly, requiring more and more cocaine to produce the same euphoric high. After repeated episodes of use over a period of several hours, the pleasurable feelings disappear. At this point the addict may abstain for a while to sleep. Twenty-four hours later the addict's tolerance for the drug will be gone, and the user finds that cocaine will again provide the euphoria he or she wants.

If the cocaine addict starts again with the dosage that he or she ended with the last time, he or she may overdose because his or her tolerance level has decreased significantly. Overdosing is also possible because of the variations that exist in the strength of any supply of cocaine. When overdose occurs the heart rate and body temperature rise to dangerous levels and may result in convulsions and even cardiac or respiratory failure leading to coma and death.[5]

HEROIN

Heroin is an opiate derived from the opium poppy mainly grown in three areas of the world: Southwest Asia (the "Golden Crescent") of Iran, Afghanistan and Pakistan; Southeast Asia (the "Golden Triangle") of Laos, Thailand and Burma; and Mexico and Colombia. "Black tar" is a cheap form of heroin from Mexico.

The most common way heroin is used is by injection, either intravenously (mainlining) or subcutaneously (skin-popping). Heroin can also be snorted. Another way of using heroin, which is popular with young people who have an aversion to needles, is smoking (chasing the dragon). A user burns a small amount of heroin on foil or a spoon and "chases" the fine spiral of smoke deep into the lungs.

Heroin is less widely used than alcohol, marijuana, or cocaine because it is feared by most potential drug users and because taking drugs by intravenous injection, as heroin is typically used, is seen by most people as a mark of depravity.

Heroin is powerfully addictive both as to its ability to enhance feelings of well-being and calmness and as a substitute for natural chemicals in the brain. Once a heroin user has experienced its effects, it becomes difficult not to use. Heroin replaces the brain's own natural opiate-like chemicals thereby causing a natural deficiency. This process encourages the user to continue to use to avoid the withdrawal symptoms that result from the deficiency.

After repeated use, heroin produces complete tolerance

to its euphoric effect; consequently, heroin addicts must raise their dose continuously to get high. Like cocaine, the effects of heroin use are of brief duration. Heroin users typically take heroin intravenously six or more times a day to keep from going into withdrawals. High-dose heroin use, in the absence of tolerance, can lead to depressed respiration and death.

Heroin addicts die from overdose deaths with some regularity. They frequently go through periods of involuntary withdrawal when they cannot get a supply of their expensive drug. When they resume heroin use, they lack tolerance. The large doses of heroin they had been taking previously with no problems can then be lethal. Another risk of overdose results from the wide fluctuations in quality that plague the street heroin market. Variations in potency can be extreme. The purity of street heroin can range from zero on the low end to 90-plus on the high end.

METHAMPHETAMINE

Methamphetamine is a synthetic drug that mimics the effects of cocaine. Meth can be produced in home laboratories in small quantities in a crystalline form. This is know as "crystal meth" or "ice." The major difference between cocaine and a synthetic stimulant like meth is that meth produces effects for many hours after a single use rather than for only a few minutes like cocaine.

Experienced meth users usually move from oral use to smoking "ice" or intravenous injection in order to produce more rapid and higher peaks of the drug in their brains. Meth produces a surge of energy and alertness and a temporary loss of appetite. There is a flash of euphoria followed by a an extended period of alertness. Because meth blocks the appetite so effectively some women use it to lose weight. The effects of meth use can fade over a period of up to eight hours. Users will frequently "chase" the high by increasing use to the point where they are smoking "ice" for days or weeks with little food or sleep.

Meth use can cause tremors, dizziness, nausea, and rapid heartbeat. One serious danger is the psycho-emotional melt-down of toxic psychosis, the symptoms of which include hallucinations, panic, paranoia, and irrational, and even violent behavior. Meth is the most chemically toxic of all the synthetic drugs. It affects all systems of the body. It often takes years for the body to recover from its harmful effects.

ECSTASY

Ecstasy, is chemically known as MDA (Methylenedioxymethamphetamine). Slang terms for ecstacy include "E", "X", "xtc", or "Adam." Ecstasy is a stimulant closely related to methamphetamine. It is popular among adolescents and young adults and primarily sold at nightclubs, bars, and all night dancing parties called "raves." It is usually ingested in tablet form but can be crushed and snorted and injected. Ecstasy produces both stimulant and psychedelic effects. It enables party-goers to dance and stay active for long periods of time. Its effects last about four to six hours.

Users describe themselves as feeling open, accepting, wholesome, beautiful, unafraid, and connected to the people around them. Typically used in social settings, Ecstasy is considered a sensuous (though not necessarily sexual) drug. Its effects are stimulated by visuals, sounds, smells, and touch.

. . . Ecstasy users' pupils dilate, often making them very sensitive to light. Jaw-clenching and tooth-grinding are also observable effects. Senses are heightened, and Ecstasy users often want to intensify the feeling by dancing, talking, and touching. Users often display overt signs of affection, which explains its nickname, the "hug drug."[6]

Rave party dancers are at risk of hyperthermia (a dangerous increase in body temperature) and heat stroke due to the combination of the drug's stimulant effect, which allows the user to dance for long periods of time, and the hot, crowded atmosphere of rave parties. Promoters of raves usually have bottled water available that the dancers can purchase and drink to avoid dehydration.

Ecstasy can cause psychological difficulties such as confusion, depression, sleep problems, and paranoia during and sometimes weeks after taking the drug. Physical symptoms can include muscle tension, involuntary teeth clenching, nausea, blurred vision, feeling faint, tremors, rapid eye movement, and sweating or chills.[7]

Although Ecstasy is not physically addictive, it can create psychological dependence or addiction. This means that the user will not suffer physical withdrawal symptoms without the drug, but will suffer psychological withdrawal symptoms, such as severe depression and anxiety. And contrary to the belief of many teenagers and youth, Ecstasy does have negative long term health effects.

Recent research findings link MDMA (Ecstasy) to long-term damage to those parts of the brain critical to thought and memory. Ecstasy impairs the function and long term production of serotonin, a brain chemical playing a role in regulating mood, memory, sleep, and appetite. Research from the National Institute on Drug Abuse shows Ecstasy causes long-lasting, possibly permanent, damage to nerve endings in the brain that are critical for thought and memory.[8]

COMMONLY ABUSED PRESCRIPTION DRUGS

Estimates are not precise as to how many Americans abuse prescription drugs.

According to the National Household Survey on Drug Abuse, nearly 9.3 million Americans reported having used prescription drugs–sedatives, tranquilizers, or pain relievers–for non-medical purposes during the year 1999.[9]

TYPE OF DRUG	NUMBER REPORTING ABUSE
Stimulants	2,302,000
Pain Relievers	6,634,000
Tranquilizers	2,793,000
Sedatives	632,000

Prescription drug abuse is often difficult to recognize. It is a private affair between the abuser and a bottle of pills. The prescription drug abuser is not subject to the social stigma of the alcoholic or drug addict. Abusers of prescription drugs see themselves as different from addicts; they often think their prescribed medication is justified even though they may be manipulative and deceptive in acquiring excessive amounts of drugs.

OPIATES. Opiates are prescribed to relieve acute pain such as may be caused by cancer or surgery. They are normally prescribed for a short period of time. In addition to blocking pain messages to the brain, they produce feelings of euphoria or pleasure. Chronic use results in tolerance and dependence. Common opiate drugs include the following:[10]

Darvocet	Methadone	Roxiprin
Darvon	Morphine	Tussionex
Demerol	OxyContin	Tylenol with
Dilaudid	Percocet	Codeine

| Lorcet | Percodan | Vicodin |
| Lortab | Roxicet | |

STIMULANTS

These drugs stimulate the central nervous system, increasing mental alertness and energy and produce a sense of well being that is accompanied with an increase in blood pressure, heart rate and respiration. These drugs are prescribed for attention deficit disorder and narcolepsy. They include Adderall, Cylert, Dexedrine and Ritalin.

CNS DEPRESSANTS. CNS depressants slow down normal brain and neurological function. In higher doses, some CNS depressants can become general anesthetics. CNS depressants can be divided into two groups, based on their chemistry and pharmacology:

- Barbiturates, such as methobarbital (Mebaral) and phenobarbital sodium (Nembutal) which are used to treat anxiety, tension, and sleep disorders.
- Benzodiazephines, such as diazepam (Valium), chlordiazepoxide HCI (Librium), and alprazolam (Xanax), which are prescribed to treat anxiety, acute stress reactions, and panic attacks. Benzodiazephines that have a more sedating effect such as triazolam (Halcion) and estazolam (ProSom) are prescribed for short-term treatment of sleep disorders.[11]

Denial is common with abusers of prescription drugs. The following is a prescription drug abuse checklist. Ask yourself the following questions about opiates, sedatives, and stimulants:[12]

- Have you been taking sleeping pills every day for more than three months?
- Have you tried to stop taking pills and felt vulnerable or frightened?
- Have you tried to stop taking pills and felt your body

start to tremble or shake?

- Do you continue to take pills even though the medical reason for taking them is no longer present?
- Do you think pills are more important than family and friends?
- Are you mixing pills with wine, liquor, or beer?
- Are you taking one kind of pill to combat the effects of another pill?
- Do you take pills to get high and have fun?
- Do you take pills when you're upset or to combat loneliness?
- Do you feel happy if your doctor writes a prescription for drugs that change your mood?
- Do you visit several doctors for the same prescription?
- Are you taking more pills to achieve the same effect you used to experience with smaller doses?
- Do you find it difficult to fulfill work obligations when you're taking pills?
- Do you ever promise yourself that you will stop taking pills and then break the promise?

If you answer "yes" or "sometimes" to three or more of these questions, you may be developing a problem with prescription drug dependence.

THE PATHWAY TO ADDICTION

No one starts drinking alcohol or using drugs believing they will become an addict. They all believe they can drink alcohol or use drugs moderately and, if necessary, will be able to quit at any time. Ask any person who drinks or uses drugs and he or she will typically respond: "It is not a problem. It is no big deal. I can control my drinking and drug use and quit any time I want to."

THE GATEWAY DRUGS

There is considerable empirical evidence for the "gateway" hypothesis that adolescents' involvement with drugs begins with alcohol and cigarettes or both. Alcohol and cigarette use by teenagers is usually underage use and illegal. The next stage of drug use is marijuana followed by cocaine, meth, and heroin. Studies strongly show that the earlier a child uses drugs, including alcohol and tobacco, the more likely he or she is to develop major addiction as an adult.[13]

ADDICTION

A person is not an addict merely because he or she is a heavy user of alcohol or drugs. Addiction should be distinguished from heavy, ill-advised, or socially unacceptable use. Many heavy users can moderate their use of alcohol or drugs—even quit completely. Addiction has two distinct features. The first feature is loss of control over the addictive behavior. This involves persistence in the addictive behavior despite problems and despite repeated efforts to stop the behavior by the addicted person and by other people. The second feature of addiction is denial and dishonesty.

Addicts continue to use alcohol and drugs despite having plenty of good reasons to stop and in the face of disastrous negative consequences. Their disease tells them that they are fine and that they do not have a problem. They are in denial, which is part of the disease.

Dr. Robert L. Dupont, a clinical professor of psychiatry at Georgetown University School of Medicine, and the first director of the National Institute of Drug Abuse, has characterized or identified three stages of addiction: (1) fooling around, (2) being hooked, and (3) hitting bottom. How rapidly a particular person moves through these stages depends on many factors, including genetic predisposition, the age when drug use begins, how quickly they fell in love with the particular drug, the particular drug involved, the frequency of use, the manner of using and whether their social environment encourages drug use, such as having a peer group or a close friend who is an addict.[14]

FOOLING AROUND

Fooling around is the honeymoon stage. The user seeks euphoria, a good feeling. He or she is experiencing new and powerful feelings and feels relaxed, more able to cope with the realities of life. Drinking and drug use is enjoyable.

Many people who fool around with alcohol or drugs decide to drop them or can drink or use socially without falling in love with them. If individuals who drink socially and in control continue to drink or use, they may have a significant change occur in their life that causes them to turn increasingly to alcohol and drugs for pleasure and to escape from problems. The fooling around stage can involve a peer group or a close friend who drinks or uses:

> Use of alcohol and drugs usually begins between the ages of twelve and twenty, with the most common starting age in North America today for the two principal gateway drugs of intoxication (alcohol and marijuana) being the ninth grade, or about age fifteen or sixteen.
>
> . . . Peer groups of heavy users of alcohol and other drugs are especially at risk. One of the top predictors of addiction is having a best friend who is an addict. Having personal values favorable to drug use and spending time with others who have the same values increase the risk of trying drugs and, once having tried them, of progressing to loss of control over drug use.[15]

Use of the gateway drugs of alcohol and marijuana usually begins in the teenage years. As use continues and users become more experienced, they branch out by using cocaine, meth and perhaps heroin depending on the current attitude of their peers. As use becomes more frequent and intense, they move along the pathway to addiction.

HOOKED

Being hooked is when the individual falls in love with alcohol or a particular drug. It can happen with lightning speed, or it can happen slowly and almost imperceptibly. The stage of falling in love, however, like all stages of addiction, is progressive. Alcohol and drugs have direct access to the brain pleasure center, and the individual controls both how much and how often he or she uses. Users lose objectivity and rational control of their lives when the drug becomes the object of their love.

As alcohol and drug use continues, tolerance develops, and more and more of the drug is used, but the "highs" get progressively lower:

> Each time drug use occurs, regardless of the sinking baseline of the feeling of well-being, there is a prompt and certain reward after drug use that is powerfully reinforcing. The brain's hardware says, "Yes, more" to the drug after every single use. The drug is a chemical lover that steals the brain's natural control mechanisms.[16]

Once an addict is hooked, all that really matters is getting the drug. The drug addict starts to ignore his friends and his family and concentrates completely on the drug and its use. Alcohol or drugs become the consuming focus or "love" of the addict's life.

HITTING BOTTOM

As an addict continues drug or alcohol use, he or she encounters very painful and inescapable consequences. A bottom may occur because of a severe auto accident, criminal arrest, imprisonment, life-threatening health problems, family disruption, financial loss, or loss of a career. If one of these particular events occurs in the life of a drug addict, he may quit for a short period of time, but soon goes back to his love affair with alcohol or drugs. Then the addict hits another bottom, perhaps lower than the last. The ultimate bottom, of course, is death.

The addict has lost control of his life. He is in denial. He is dishonest with himself and others. Alcoholics and drug addicts are liars. The use of alcohol and drugs always leads to lying because the negative consequences and the abnormality of the behavior caused by the addiction are inescapable.

As addicts hit bottom, they desperately try to gain control of their lives, but without giving up the use of alcohol or drugs. Many times addicts abstain temporarily from using. They will "white knuckle" abstinence, but they are angry and resentful of being deprived of alcohol or drugs that are the primary focus of their lives.

Recovery cannot begin until the addict truly believes that he or she cannot gain control of life and still drink or use and that he or she will continue to sink to lower and lower bottoms with even more serious consequences, which may include death.

Elder Boyd K. Packer has summarized the pathway to addiction as follows:

> Then many of them turn elsewhere, seeking to escape the futility in life. They turn to drugs and find for a moment the escape they seek. At last their spirits soar. They reach beyond themselves, erase all limitations, and taste for a moment, as they suppose, that which they have been seeking. But it a synthetic, a wicked counterfeit, for they return to a depression worse than the one they left. Then they become players in the saddest of human tragedies.

For, as they turn again to this release, they are not seeking what they sought before, but indulge to escape the consequences of each previous adventure with drugs. This is addiction! This is tragedy! This is slavery![17]

3

The Personal and Social Carnage of Alcohol and Drug Addiction

The personal and social carnage of alcoholism and drug addiction are staggering. Addiction is like a tornado leaving nothing but destruction and death in its path. Millions of lives are scarred by violence, disease, poverty, and the incalculable individual pain of addiction.

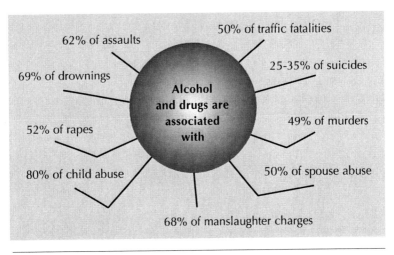

62% of assaults

50% of traffic fatalities

69% of drownings

25-35% of suicides

Alcohol and drugs are associated with

52% of rapes

49% of murders

80% of child abuse

50% of spouse abuse

68% of manslaughter charges

Substance abuse does not occur in a vacuum.[3]

Most addicts have lost their spouse, their children, their employment, their home, their self respect, and many times, their health. They are emotionally and spiritually bankrupt.

Addicts feel totally disempowered because of uncontrolled drinking or drug use and the behavior that results. They are no longer in charge of their life.

SUBSTANCE ABUSE DOES NOT OCCUR IN A VACUUM

Nearly one-half of all traffic accidents are alcohol related. Alcohol related traffic accidents are the leading cause of death in adolescents. Alcohol related accidents and illnesses combined are the second leading cause of premature death, exceeded only by tobacco. Each year 115,000 people die from alcohol abuse and 30,000 from illegal drugs.

Each year 1.7 million people are victims of alcohol related crimes and over 4,000 people die from such crimes.[1] The number of deaths annually from illegal drugs in Utah has risen dramatically in the last decade, from 20 in 1991, to 130 in 1998, to 148 in 2001.[2]

DAVID AND ROBERTA'S STORY. David was 21 and Roberta was 19. They were friends. They "hung out" together. David was a drug addict and was taking methadone to come off his heroin addiction. He had some methadone that had been prescribed by a rehabilitation facility. One evening David and Roberta were at David's home in his bedroom, and Roberta saw the bottle of methadone on David's dresser. The bottle was labeled "poison" and that taking methadone could be fatal. Roberta told David that she would like a "taste" of the methadone. David gave her a "taste." That evening Roberta swallowed about 100 milligrams of methadone, the entire bottle. But David wasn't worried because he thought that Roberta would "sleep it off," and he was going to watch her during the night. Although David observed Roberta having difficulty breathing, he did not call 911 until after she had stopped breathing. By the time Roberta reached the hospital, she had gone into full cardiac arrest and was in a coma. She died three days later. David was charged with manslaughter, a second degree felony; he recklessly caused Roberta's death. He was also charged with the possession of a controlled substance. Just prior to trial, he entered a plea agreement, pleading no contest to manslaughter and guilty to possession of heroin. He was sentenced to eighteen months in the county jail, twelve months on the manslaughter charge and six months on the possession of heroin charge, with the sentences to run concurrently.

ALCOHOL AND DRUGS AND THE PRISON POPULATION

Because of crimes associated with alcohol and drug abuse, we continue to build more and more prisons and jails. In 1996, Americans paid $38 billion in taxes to build and operate 4,700 prisons—1,403 state, 82 federal and 3,304 local.[4]

More than 1.8 million individuals are behind bars in America: 1,130,000 in state prisons, 568,000 in local jails and 113,000 in federal prisons. Eighty percent— 1,450,000 inmates—either violated drug or alcohol laws, were high at the time of their offense, stole property to buy drugs, have histories of drug and alcohol abuse and addiction, or share some mix of these characteristics. Tragically, among these 1,450,000 inmates are the parents of 2.4 million children.[5]

The number of drug offenders sentenced to state prisons has increased nearly 12-fold, from 9,000 in 1980 to 107,000 in 1998. In the year 2000 the United States had two million of its citizens behind bars. With 5% of the world's population, the United States has 25% of the world's prisoners.[6]

TRAVIS' STORY. Travis grew up in a home with an alcoholic abusive father. His parents divorced when he was about sixteen. Travis struggled with an anger problem and he took several anger management classes in high school. He was a star high school football player and received a university football scholarship. Along with his anger problem, Travis also had an alcohol problem. By the time he was a freshman in college he was a heavy drinker. He had come to believe that alcohol made things better and made problems go away. One night at a drinking party Travis got into a minor altercation with a teenage boy, Paul. Travis had a baseball bat and he hit Paul on the head with such force that the bat broke. Paul suffered multiple skull fractures, intracranial bleeding, and several broken teeth. The doctors were amazed that Paul was still alive. Travis was arrested and charged with attempted murder, a second degree felony, and aggravated assault, a third degree felony. Upon the Court dismissing the attempted murder charge, Travis pled guilty to the aggravated assault charge. He was sentenced to an indeterminate sentence of not more than five years in the state prison.

Behind each alcohol and drug related crime, with its attendant economic cost, are the personal and tragic stories of those who are addicted to alcohol or drugs, their family, and the innocent victims.

The following describe a few of the personal but common tragedies:

- Addicted parents, when given a choice between getting treatment or losing their children to state custody, choose to remain on drugs.
- Returned missionaries, divorced, with children, incarcerated because of cocaine, heroin, or amphetamine use.
- Fetal alcohol syndrome which is caused by a mother's drinking during pregnancy results in tens of thou-

sands of babies being born each year with incurable mental handicaps.

- Newly born children who cannot be nurtured by their mother because she is serving a three year sentence for a crack cocaine use.
- Men and women whose minds have been "blown out" because of extended drug use.
- A homeless young mother, a meth addict, living with her two children under a viaduct.
- Addicts who commit suicide because the pain is too great and there is no hope and no way out.
- A college coed at a party who gets drunk and passes out and then is gang raped by a group of drunken fraternity brothers.
- A husband and wife, cocaine addicts, who start their pre-teenage children on drugs.
- The drug addict or alcoholic who is now mentally or physically disabled as a result of a failed suicide attempt.
- The 22-year-old father who is now a paraplegic because a drunk driver ran a red light.

The above stories could be multiplied thousands of times over and would not even scratch the surface of the personal tragedies caused by alcohol and drugs. There are thousands of Church members that are on the addiction path that is leading them to personal tragedies similar to or as devastating as those described above. This can be avoided with proper intervention and treatment. It is not necessary for an addict to hit his lowest bottom before he enters treatment. Church leaders and members knowledgeable about addiction and available treatment options can detour many Church members off their addiction path and save them from untold pain and loss.

4
Condemnation or Compassion and Unconditional Love?

Whether or not you believe that alcoholism or drug addiction are diseases or the result of a moral failure of willpower, alcoholics and drug addicts are in desperate need of help. They have lost everything that our society values. They live in guilt, shame, loneliness, and indescribable emotional and physical pain. They have tried numerous times to get clean and sober and each time they have failed. They are desperate for compassion, understanding, love and help. Remember the words of the Savior:

> For I was an hungered, and ye gave me meat: I was thirsty, and ye gave me drink: I was a stranger, and ye took me in: Naked and ye clothed me: I was sick, and ye visited me: I was in prison, and ye came unto me. Then shall the righteous answer him, saying, Lord, when saw we thee an hungered, and fed thee? Or thirsty, and gave thee drink? When saw we a stranger, and took thee in? Or naked, and clothed thee? Or when saw we sick, or in prison, and came unto thee? And the King shall answer and say unto them, Verily I say unto you, Inasmuch as ye have done it unto one of the least of these my brethren, ye have done it unto me (Matt. 25:35-40).

Alcoholics and drug addicts are certainly "an hungered," "strangers," "naked," "sick," or, "imprisoned."

If we would show compassion to the Savior, we must show compassion to the addict. Matthew J. Cowley, an apostle of The Church of Jesus Christ Latter-day Saints, had a great respect for the program of Alcoholics Anonymous and its message and mission. He loved all men and women whether they were alcoholic or non-alcoholic. In speaking about Alcoholics Anonymous Elder Cowley said:

> There isn't anything I can say that is too good about this great organization. I have attended the meetings, I am always glad to give what support I can. . . . Now there is one thing I have learned, and it has been a wonderful thing for me as a religionist in my present position. I've learned from these men that there isn't a man living who isn't greater than his sins, who isn't greater than his weaknesses. That's a wonderful thing to know. It is a wonderful thing to know that, even though a man may sink so low that he is at the bottom of the gutter, yet within him there is a greatness that can regenerate him if he will submit himself to the right influences and to the power above and beyond himself.[1]

> So, brothers and sisters, let's be very kind to one another. None of us has lived his life yet. We don't know what the morrow is going to bring, you know. Men who haven't touched a drop (of alcohol) today may next year be alcoholics. Men who are alcoholics today may in a couple of years from now be bishops of the South 18th Ward. You can never tell. That's the Gospel of Jesus Christ. We should always keep in mind that two of the most glorious principles in this Church are—repentance and forgiveness.[2]

It is not easy to love or forgive an alcoholic or drug addict, particularly when your life has been devastated by

his or her active addiction, or you have been a helpless victim of drunk driving or criminal acts. Nevertheless, the
Savior expects us to love and forgive the addict and his or
her trespasses:

> Wherefore, I say unto you, that ye ought to forgive one
> another; for he that forgiveth not his brother his tres-
> passes standeth condemned before the Lord; for there
> remaineth in him the greater sin. I, the Lord, will forgive
> whom I will forgive, but of you it is required to forgive
> all men (D&C 64:9,10).

The Prophet Joseph Smith taught:

> The nearer we get to our Heavenly Father, the more we
> are disposed to look with compassion on perishing
> souls; we feel that we want to take them upon our shoul-
> ders, and cast their sins behind our backs.[3]

Alcoholics and drug addicts are plagued by low self-
esteem, a sense of aloneness, guilt, fear, shame and anxiety.
Many of those affiliated with the Church have been excommunicated or disfellowshipped. Many, at a young age, just
"turned their back on the Church and walked away." They
have hopes of being rebaptized and being brought back into
full fellowship and enjoy the blessings of the gospel. They
need the hand of friendship and fellowship. They need the
arms of love and acceptance.

At a Regional Conference held in September, 2002,
President Gordon B. Hinckley said that he was getting old
and that he was not going to live forever. He said: "I wonder
what I can leave with you as a last testament." He men-
tioned several things. He spoke of an addict that had been
converted and then he said: "Don't shun these people. Don't
let them sit all day by themselves. Love them. They may not
be dressed the way you think they ought to be. They may not

smell like you think they ought to. Love them. Be a friend. Walk beside them."[4]

Phil S., a recovering alcoholic, in his book, T*he Perfect Brightness of Hope*, expressed his feelings as he came back to Church as follows:

> Because I smelled of alcohol and tobacco, many Church members shunned me. I can appreciate how lepers in olden times must have felt. With the exception of a few persistent Christians, I experienced little welcome. But I was determined to attend Church regardless of what others thought. I would sometimes smoke a cigarette in the Church parking lot, take a drink of whiskey, and then go into the chapel like a fire-breathing dragon. I didn't do this to impress or annoy anyone. Knowing I was unworthy and as an excommunicated member, I never partook of the sacrament. This behavior was simply me during that part of my life. I received many nonverbal, and a few verbal, rebukes from the saints sitting near me. But I was spiritually starving to death. I wanted to again feel the inner peace associated with a life in harmony with the Gospel. I knew if I waited until I smelled better, I would never get back my spiritual health.[5]

After a Church Substance Abuse missionary had explained the LDS 12-Step Addiction Recovery Program, a member said, "Well, I don't know why you would want to be involved with "those people." The reason is that "those people" are our brothers and sisters. The Savior ministered to lepers and sinners—to "those people." Such a statement by a member indicates that he or she does not understand the basic principles of the gospel. Charity, or the pure love of Christ, is at the center of the gospel of Jesus Christ. "Wherefore my beloved brethren if ye have not charity, ye are nothing" (Mor. 7:46).

As we think about our attitudes toward the addict, we should reflect upon the parable of the prodigal son. A father's youngest son took his inheritance and went "into a far country and wasted his substance with riotous living." He finally hit bottom as he was eating husks with the swine:

> He arose, and came to his father. But when he was yet a great way off, his father saw him, and had compassion, and ran, and fell on his neck, and kissed him. But the father said to his servants, Bring forth the best robe, and put it on him; and put a ring on his hand, and shoes on his feet. And bring hither the fatted calf, and kill it; and let us eat, and be merry; for this my son was dead, and is alive again; he was lost, and is found. And they began to be merry (Luke 15:20, 22-24).

Addicts are prodigal sons and daughters of Heavenly Father. They have "wasted their substance" in a far country called "addiction." Those seeking help have "come to themselves" and have decided to come home. Will we, like the father in the parable, greet the addict with joy and give him our robe and place a ring on his finger? Do we have an attitude of forgiveness toward the returning addict? "For he that forgiveth not his brother . . . there remaineth in him the greater sin" (D& C 64:9). Mahatma Gandhi wisely said: "The weak can never forgive, forgiveness is an attribute of the strong."

Many alcoholics or drug addicts waste years and decades of their lives in their addiction. Periods of sobriety are followed by relapse and probably a lower bottom than the last. They have not spent years of labor and service in the Church, but instead have spent years in bars and "crack" houses. Many die along the way, but many also make it out of the morass of alcohol and drugs and want to join with the fellowship of the saints. They come late into the vineyard to labor.

In the parable of the laborers in the vineyard some workers started early in the morning; others came during the day, and some came into the vineyard only at the eleventh hour. When the householder paid all of the laborers the same, many complained:

> These last have wrought but one hour, and thou hast made them equal unto us, which have borne the burden and heat of the day (Matt. 20:12).

Elder Dallin H. Oaks, in discussing the parable of the laborers in the vineyard, comments on the objections of those who had "borne the burden and heat of the day:"

> The Master's reward in the Final Judgment will not be based on how long we have labored in the vineyard. We do not obtain our heavenly reward by punching a time clock. What is essential is that our labors in the workplace of the Lord have caused us to *become* something. For some of us, this requires a longer time than for others. What is important in the end is what we have become by our labors. Many who come in the eleventh hour have been refined and prepared by the Lord in ways other than formal employment in the vineyard (emphasis added).[6]

GENERAL NEGATIVE PUBLIC ATTITUDE

There is a general negative public attitude toward assisting those whose lives have been devastated by addiction. Government and public support for the funding of treatment facilities is low. A leader of the Eagle Forum, a conservative group, was reported as saying, "We shouldn't expect the average citizen to pay for people who have gotten themselves in these messes. It's not right and it is not the proper role of government."[7]

The foregoing attitude is very short sighted, both from

an economic standpoint and from a crime reduction stand-point. A two-year California Drug and Alcohol Assessment showed that for every $1.00 spent on alcohol and drug treatment, $7.14 was saved in future costs, largely in relation to costs avoided because of reductions in crime.[7]

In June 1994, the Rand Corporation released a study that compared certain methods that would reduce cocaine use in the United States by an estimated 1%:[8]

- source country control—$783 million
- interdiction at the borders—$366 million
- domestic law enforcement—$246 million
- drug treatment—$34 million

Despite the huge difference in the cost to reduce drug use through drug treatment, there are not enough treatment facilities available to treat all the people who need and want to get into treatment programs. It is estimated that in the United States there are 2,603,000 treatment slots needed, in addition to the 950,000 that already exist.[9] Tragically, in September, 2002, the Salvation Army in Salt Lake City announced the closure of its 108 bed alcohol and drug addiction facility because of lack of government funding and charitable contributions.[10]

5

Treatment and Recovery

There is no medical cure for alcohol or drug addiction. The disease of addiction can be brought into remission, through the process called "recovery." Recovery is more than abstinence from alcohol and drugs. It is learning how to live life and cope with all of its stresses and challenges without alcohol or drugs. This is not an easy task for one who has relied on alcohol or drugs for many years. The addict must have self-compassion while avoiding self-pity. "Compassion for self enables the patient to appropriately mourn the very real losses substance abuse has inflicted and to move to an enjoyable sobriety."[1]

The nature of the disease of addiction results in addicts experiencing multiple cycles of treatment, abstinence, and relapse. Parents of teenage addicts are shocked to learn that one three-week rehabilitation program has not "fixed" their son or daughter. Relapse is part of the disease of addiction and recovery is an ongoing process rather than an end point.[2]

Although addicts do not have control over whether or not they will continue to use alcohol or illicit drugs, they do have a moral responsibility to secure treatment for their addiction. Most addicts do not seek treatment until they hit rock bottom or until they are somehow forced, perhaps by an employer or family member, to seek treatment. Of course, it would be much better if heavy users of alcohol or drugs sought treatment before they had full-blown addictions. Unfortunately, most addicts refuse treatment until their bodies, minds, and spirits have been devastated by their addictive illnesses.

The majority of addicts are poly-addicted; that is to say, they are addicted to alcohol and one or more illicit drugs and usually nicotine. Some addicts will tell you that it is harder to conquer the addiction to smoking than it is to conquer the addiction to alcohol or drugs.

Before treatment can begin, the addict must first admit to himself or herself the addiction and the need for help. Otherwise, it is doubtful that the addict will seek treatment or that any treatment will be helpful. Alcoholics and drug addicts deny, conceal, rationalize, minimize, and blame others for their addictive condition. The addict must admit that he or she is powerless over alcohol or drugs and that his or her life has become unmanageable. Addicts must give up the illusion that they can handle addictive substances and can, through their own willpower and effort, overcome their addictions.

Once an addict admits that he or she is powerless over his or her addictive disease and desires help and treatment, it then becomes necessary for the addict, his family, or friends to assist in securing the necessary professional treatment which will lead to recovery. Because alcoholism and drug addiction are multi-faceted problems with multi-faceted causes, they require professional diagnosis to determine which treatment will be effective in bringing the addictive disease into remission.

Where does one start to find help? You can find the names, addresses, and phone numbers of local alcoholic and drug treatment centers and facilities by looking in the yellow pages under the section "Alcoholism Information and Treatment" or "Drug Abuse Information and Treatment." Many of these treatment facilities offer a free initial evaluation and consultation. Most counties have a substance-abuse department which may also offer screening and referral services and are a source for obtaining a list of available local alcoholism and drug treatment facilities.

THE PROBLEM OF DUAL DIAGNOSIS

Many alcoholics and drug addicts also have psychiatric disorders that complicate their diagnosis and treatment. This situation is referred to as "dual-diagnosis," or comorbidity. These psychiatric or mental problems can include depression, bi-polar disorder, anxiety disorders, schizophrenia, attention deficit hyperactivity disorder (ADHD), and anti-social or borderline personality.

A recent nationwide survey found that nearly half of people suffering from alcohol abuse or dependence had another lifetime psychiatric diagnosis. Twenty-one percent were illicit drug abusers, and 30% had other disorders, including major depression, bipolar disorder, schizophrenia, generalized anxiety, panic attacks, and antisocial or borderline personality. Psychiatric symptoms are especially common during periods of heavy drinking. . . . Some alcoholic drinking is a misguided attempt to treat anxiety or depression. Eventually alcohol dependence and the associated anxiety, depression, or personality disorder may reinforce each other in a way that makes cause and effect difficult to distinguish.[3]

According to the *Journal of the American Medical Association,* thirty-seven percent of all people who abuse alcohol and fifty-three percent of all people who abuse drugs also have some type of emotional or mental illness.[4]

Many treatment centers are not equipped to deal with dual diagnosis patients. This is a serious problem that has not as yet been fully addressed by the medical community. Typically treatment for mental illness is at one facility and treatment for substance abuse is at another. Patients are "referred back and forth between them in what some have called 'ping-pong' therapy. What is needed are 'hybrid' programs that address both illnesses together."[5]

J.B.'S STORY. I began having anxiety attacks and depression in high school. We had moved to a new house and school district. I felt lonely and alienated, even though I was active in music programs and student government. Although I knew something was wrong, my counselors were unable to properly diagnose my problem.

My LDS mission in a predominantly Catholic country was very difficult. Upon arriving at the mission home, I had my first full-blown anxiety attack. I was full of dread and couldn't breathe or move. I felt detached from my body. The anxiety and depression continued my whole mission.

My college years contained more of the same distress. While I drank before my mission, I started drinking excessively to ward off anxiety. Exams or work stress seemed easier to handle with alcohol. After seeing many counselors, I still had not been diagnosed with clinical depression.

At 23 I married, and my addiction and depression continued. This was compounded with many job moves and marital conflict. At 31, in my first rehab, I was dual diagnosed with depression and alcoholism. I was prescribed with antidepressants that I continue to take after nine years.

My experience in multiple rehabilitation programs and hundreds of Alcoholics Anonymous meetings, tells me that most addicts have dual diagnosis which is biologically and psychologically based. Both should be treated at the same time. Mentally ill patients that are treated only for substance abuse stand a high potential for relapse.

One must realize that removing drugs only allows the brain and nervous system to begin to heal. Ongoing treatment should include nutritional supplements, diet and exercise, as well as emotional and spiritual support groups. Also, removing addictive chemicals without addressing underlying psychological problems will only produce a "dry drunk." Addicts need to find a treatment center that focuses on dual diagnosis therapy. At a minimum, outside psychiatric medical treatment should be combined with addiction treatment.

My mental illness, addiction, and bad choices have cost me my temple marriage, home, job, life savings, and health. Addiction is "cunning, baffling, and powerful." All available treatments and resources should be used to combat it. Through the grace of God, I have confronted and defeated many of my demons. With His power, I will have the strength to continue my daily recovery and future progress.

INTERVENTION

Before any treatment can begin, the addict must admit he has a serious alcohol or drug problem and that he needs help. Because denial is an inherent part of the disease of addiction it is very powerful and difficult to overcome. Addicts typically deny that they have a problem or that they need treatment. Addiction is a chronic and progressive disease and without treatment it gets worse. Family members often believe that it will get better. However, a brief period of sobriety is not recovery.

When an addict does not seek treatment on his or her own, an "intervention" should be considered by family members, friends, or a therapist. An "intervention" is a planned event in which the addict is confronted in an effort to get him or her into treatment immediately.

Professional advice as to how and when to have the intervention is critical. It has to be carefully planned if it is to be successful. A successful intervention means immediately driving the addict to a waiting treatment facility. Strategies for countering all of the objections of the addict must be planned for in advance.

SUBSTANCE ABUSE TREATMENT

Substance abuse treatment teaches addicts how to function without alcohol or drugs, how to handle cravings, how to avoid situations that would lead to the use of alcohol or drugs, and also how to avoid relapse. In addition, addicts are taught how improve their personal relationships and ability to function at work and in the community.

The specific treatment model used varies from facility to facility. Group therapy is the "core treatment modality" that is used. However, individual therapy is usually also part of the treatment. There are some issues that a patient may not want to address in a group setting.

The treatment program typically involves education about the disease concept of addiction, motivational enhancement therapy, anger management, relapse prevention, the learning of life skills, and cognitive behavior skills. Motivational enhancement therapy strives to motivate the patient to use his or her own resources to change behavior. Cognitive behavior techniques teach the patient to distinguish between rational and irrational responses to events in his life, and that irrational responses can lead to relapse. The 12-step model is usually part of the treatment program. The patients work the twelve steps under the direction of a therapist.

DETOXIFICATION

The first stage of treatment is detoxification. Detoxification is defined as the process of eliminating alcohol or the illicit drug from the addict's body. This process is necessary to protect the health or even the life of the addict:

> The most common alcohol withdrawal symptoms are tremors, nausea, dry mouth, sweating, weakness and depression. The symptoms usually appear hours after sudden withdrawal, become most intense on the first day, and subside in a few days to a week. In especially severe cases, delirium tremens begin two days after withdrawal; its symptoms include high fever, a high heart rate, and sometimes hallucinations or seizures.[6]

Withdrawal from cocaine and amphetamines can result in a very deep depression known as a crash. This can lead to another addictive cycle or suicide. Withdrawal from opiates feels like a bad case of the flu but is not as dangerous as withdrawal from depressants such as alcohol.

Detoxification can be accomplished at inpatient rehabilitation facilities that have trained medical personnel or those facilities that have immediate access to medical personnel. Detox facilities can be located through the yellow pages under the headings of "Alcoholism Information & Treatment" or "Drug Abuse Information & Treatment" or by contacting a county substance abuse department.

Many alcoholics and drug addicts end up in hospital emergency rooms where detoxification starts, and they can receive medical care and the necessary prescriptions to ease withdrawals. Pursuant to the Federal Emergency Medical Treatment and Labor Act (EMTLA), all hospitals that participate in the Medicare program must provide "stabilizing care" for a patient with an emergency condition and provide the care and appropriate transfer to another facility even if the person has no insurance or ability to pay. Approximately one-fourth of all emergency hospital admissions are related to the treatment of alcohol related problems.[7] After an alcoholic or drug addict is detoxified, the patient has a number of different treatment options. The selection of a particular treatment should be made with the assistance of a medical consultant or professional. Alcoholism and drug abuse treatment can be performed in an in-patient, residential or outpatient facility. Generally before admission into a treatment facility, the patient must be clean and sober for seven days.

PATIENT EVALUATION

Patient evaluation is a process to determine placement of a patient in a specific level (intensity) of care. Levels of care from outpatient services (low intensity) to medically managed (high intensity) inpatient services. The most commonly used patient placement criteria is that developed by the American Society of Addiction Medicine (ASAM). Most county substance abuse departments have substance abuse assessment and referral specialists who can evaluate a patient's particular needs and recommend what level of treatment care would be most appropriate.

INPATIENT TREATMENT

Inpatient treatment involves a more or less prolonged stay in a treatment program that is medically managed. The length of stay is typically 28 days. Detoxification of the alcoholic or drug addict can be medically managed. The medical staff can also diagnose and treat an addict who has the problem of "dual diagnosis", ie. psychiatric or mental problems (such as depression, anxiety, bi-polar disorder or schizophrenia) in addition to addiction.

RESIDENTIAL TREATMENT

Treatment in a residential facility is less structured and intensive than inpatient treatment. The treatment period is generally 30 to 90 days. The on-site staff does not include physicians or psychiatrists. These are brought into the facility as needed so that patients can receive psychiatric evaluation and psychotherapy.

In a somewhat less intensive residential program, the patient resides and has his meals at the treatment facility but the patient, after a certain time period, with a pass, can leave during the afternoon and evening. Patients are encouraged and sometimes required to secure part-time employment in the afternoon and early evening. The length of stay at this type of program can be from 90 days to a year or more. This program has the advantage of assisting the patient to make the transition from treatment to normal work-a-day living. Some counties may provide low cost housing to the patient after he has completed the program.

JIM'S STORY. Jim was a cocaine addict. This was Jim's fourth rehab program. He had been at the house for about two months. Group therapy was in the morning. Each patient met with a counselor once a week. From noon until the 10:00 p.m. curfew was free time. Patients were expected to get a part-time job in the afternoon or evening. Jim had been trying to get a job but without any success. One night Jim did not check in by curfew time. The following day two patients got permission to take the van and go out and try to find Jim. This was futile. Two days elapsed and then the following morning Jim's obituary appeared in the newspaper. Jim had been found by the police under some bushes, dead from a cocaine overdose. The next day a memorial service was held for Jim at the house. It was a somber affair. Jim was a good guy.

OUTPATIENT TREATMENT

Intensive outpatient treatment typically involves the patient in treatment at a facility for three to four hours a night, three to five times a week, usually for eight weeks. This allows the patient to remain employed and at home during treatment. Less intensive outpatient treatment would involve fewer than nine hours a week. Outpatient treatment usually involves both group and individual sessions with a therapist. Currently the majority of addicts are treated in outpatient facilities, primarily because of the lower cost of treatment.

OPIATE MAINTENANCE TREATMENT

Addicts to heroin and other opiates can be given methadone as a long-lasting opiate substitute. Methadone reduces the craving for heroin and prevents withdrawal symptoms. This allows the patient to take advantage of psychosocial treatment. Methadone treatment is administered through clinics on a highly-regulated basis. LAAM is another long-lasting opiate that also provides stability for the addict. However, methadone is preferred by addicts. Buprenorphine was recently approved by the Federal Drug Administration as an additional intervention for opiate addiction.

Methadone at times produces a light high and makes the addict feel normal. LAAM produces a more level state. Methadone treatment can vary from gradually decreasing the dosage until the patient is completely off methadone or long-term methadone use that continues for years.

The initial hope of practitioners, policymakers and regulators was that methadone could be used to transition patients to a drug-free lifestyle and then be withdrawn. This has not proved to be the case. Repeated studies suggest that only 10% to 20% of patients who discontinue methadone are able to remain abstinent.[8]

There is substantial criticism of methadone treatment on the grounds that it merely replaces one drug with another.

This is certainly the view of attendees at Alcoholics Anonymous and Narcotics Anonymous.

GINGER'S STORY. When I was in college I started using cocaine. It gave me a surge of energy and suppressed my appetite. I liked using it because it helped me stay thin. I snorted cocaine for many years. I would stop for short periods of time only to relapse. Sometime along the way I started snorting crystal meth. Meth was my "dream drug," and it lasted much longer than cocaine.

One time when I was trying to get clean, I took a friend to a few LDS Substance Abuse Recovery meetings. She said I should try heroin, "It is really good." I resisted at first, because I feared heroin, but I finally started to use it. I "mainlined" the heroin. It was different than meth. Heroin had a very euphoric calming effect. I continued using heroin for two years. My veins became so scarred that it was difficult for me to "mainline," so I started snorting or smoking the heroin until my veins worked again. I also started doing something very dangerous: shooting "speed balls," a mixture of heroin and cocaine.

When I was using, I felt very guilty and not worthy to pray. I remember receiving a blessing from a LDS Substance Abuse Recovery missionary. It was very different than other blessings that I had received: it was a blessing of warning. I became very frightened. I thought that I could break my heroin addiction by clinically supervised methadone treatment. Methadone helps reduce the cravings and the terrible withdrawals from heroin. The clinic started me on 30 milligrams of methadone each day. This is the starting dosage for heroin addicts. However, I was still having withdrawals, so the clinic upped my dosage to 64 milligrams a day. My supervised dosage is now declining one milligram per week.

RELAPSE AND AFTERCARE

Many individuals have the unreasonable expectation that after an alcoholic or drug addict goes through an intensive inpatient or outpatient program that he or she is "fixed" and that the problem with alcohol or illicit drugs is over. Nothing could be further from the truth. After a drug addict or alcoholic becomes clean and sober or goes through residential, intensive inpatient, or outpatient treatment, they are not automatically transformed into a normal, functioning person. Relapse is part of the disease of addiction. It is unreasonable to expect the alcoholic or drug addict to retain a life-long abstinence with his or her first treatment experience. Recovery is a difficult and painful process, fraught with the danger of relapse.

> Figuring out why addicts are so prone to relapse is a major area of research. One culprit is the phenomenon of craving, or the powerful "hunger" for drugs that can linger months or years after an addict quits using. Scientists have discovered evidence that this craving may be partly a physiological phenomenon, related to the long-term changes in brain function that addiction causes. Now accustomed to functioning in the presence of drugs, the addicted brain, in essence, has become unable to function normally in their absence. Craving is also partly a conditioned response to powerful cues to use drugs that the recovering addict may encounter—people, places, and things associated with drug use.

> . . . The best evidence available suggests that most relapses occur at times of emotional distress. It is in the presence of depression, anxiety, anger, boredom, loneliness, stress, and distress that humans are at their emotional and psychological weak point.[8]

Treatment centers teach relapse prevention skills such as identifying high risk situations, learning and rehearsing relapse prevention skills, and coping with cravings. Many treatment programs offer aftercare as part of their treatment package. This usually involves group therapy once a week to reinforce what was taught during treatment and to help the individual avoid relapse. Participation in a 12-step program is good aftercare or maintenance.

Although recovery may be a long process, it is possible. Tens of thousands of addicts have recovered, have enjoyed many years of sobriety, and have rebuilt their lives. However, the recovery time of alcohol and drug addiction is not measured in days or weeks, but in years and decades. They must accept the fact that recovery is a life-long process. The addict and his family must never give up hope and stop trying.

> The greatest danger for addicted people and their families is not that they might fail to find the best addiction treatment, it is that they are all too likely to stop treatment and to stop participation in Twelve Step programs too soon. Once they are not in treatment and/or not going to meetings, many addicted people relapse to their old addictive behavior patterns. This painful reality does not mean that addiction treatment and Twelve Step programs do not work, it means that the disease of addiction is powerful and lifelong. Only a lifelong program of recovery is likely to succeed, in the long run, for most addicts and their families.[10]

THE POST-ACUTE WITHDRAWAL SYNDROME

Researchers estimate that between 75 and 95 percent of recovering alcoholics experience lingering dysfunction related to the damage that alcohol has done to their body and brain. These problems are known as post-acute withdrawal, or the protracted withdrawal syndrome, and may last for many months. These include:

- Disrupted thought patterns, difficulty concentrating, problems with abstract reasoning and circular or obsessive thoughts.
- Memory gaps, short-term memory loss, inability to remember past significant events and difficulty learning new skills.
- Emotional hypersensitivity and emotional reactions.
- Sleep problems, such as nightmares, general restlessness and fragmented sleep.
- Physical coordination problems, such as dizziness, lack of balance and hand-eye coordination, and slow reflexes.[11]

COURT ORDERED TREATMENT

Drug courts were first started in the United States in 1989 as an alternative to incarceration. In drug court, the offender undergoes extensive supervision and treatment and regular court appearances. In 2002 there were about 1100 drug courts operating in the United States.[12] Studies show that drug courts are cost effective. In Utah, incarcerating an individual costs between $20,000 and $30,000 per year. In contrast, the cost of putting a single offender through a drug court program is $3,500.[13]

In drug court, a felony guilty plea is entered and held in abeyance until successful completion of the program. When the individual graduates from drug court, the guilty pleas are withdrawn and the criminal charges dismissed. A drug court program is usually a maximum of fifty-two weeks. To graduate, participants are given random drug tests and must be clean from all drugs for the last six months of the program.

Addicts who are not involved in criminal activity to support their habit find it difficult, if not impossible, to get into a public-funded treatment facility because they are overcrowded with criminal addicts ordered there by the courts. On occasion you will hear a jail inmate say he allowed himself to get caught and sentenced to jail so that he could have an opportunity to go to drug court and be ordered into a drug treatment facility.

Drug court, which involves sentencing a convicted drug addict to a drug treatment facility rather than incarceration, has been effective in reducing prisoner recidivism.

Accepting addiction as a brain disease also means that society should stop simplistically viewing criminal justice and health approaches as incompatible opposites. We know that between 50 percent and 70 percent of those arrested are addicted to illegal drugs. Studies indicate that if addicted offenders are provided with well-structured drug treatment while under criminal justice control, their recidivism rates can be reduced by 50 percent to 60 percent for subsequent drug use and by more than 40 percent for further criminal behavior.[14]

Recent research on recidivism of Utah drug court graduates shows that 18 months after graduation, only 15.4% had new arrests for drug-related crimes—whereas, 64% of those who did not participate in the program had new drug related arrests.[15]

COST OF TREATMENT

No generalized statement can be made about the cost of treatment, except to say that it is very expensive. Only a small percentage of addicts have insurance that will pay for treatment. Any insurance coverage for inpatient treatment is usually limited to 30 days. Outpatient coverage usually covers a longer period. Sometimes insurance will pay part or all of the cost of detoxification. Veterans have some benefits for the payment of alcohol and drug addiction treatment through the Veterans Administration. The V.A. hospital in Salt Lake City, Utah, which is a regional hospital, has addiction treatment facilities.

The high cost of treatment and the lack of government or charitable funding for treatment centers, prevents a large percentage of addicts from getting treatment. Currently more than 20,000 Utahns are in government-supported treatment plans, and an estimated 2,000 more are paying for treatment themselves in private clinics. There are about 80,000 who need treatment, but are not receiving it.[16]

Members of the Church who are addicts and their families are caught in this same economic bind. It is not uncommon for an addict to go through four or five treatment programs and then still relapse. Even though individual and extended family financial resources become totally exhausted, treatment is still needed. At this point it is appropriate for the addict and his family to seek financial help from the Church through their bishop.

6
LDS Twelve Step
Addiction Recovery Program

The LDS 12-step Addiction Recovery Program is patterned after Alcoholics Anonymous, both with respect to the twelve steps and as to meeting format. Alcoholics Anonymous was founded in 1935 in Akron, Ohio as a result of a meeting between Bill W., a New York stock broker, and Dr. Bob S., an Akron surgeon, both of whom were alcoholics. They started to work with alcoholics in the Akron City Hospital. Bill W. and Dr. Bob and one other recovering alcoholic were the nucleus of the first AA group. In the fall of 1935, a second group of recovering alcoholics was formed in New York City, and a third in Cleveland, Ohio in 1939.

In 1939, AA's basic textbook, *Alcoholics Anonymous*, (the "Big Book") was published. Written by Bill W., this book explains "How It (the twelve Steps) Works", and AA's philosophy. It also contains many personal success stories of recovering alcoholics. The book, Twelve Steps and Twelve Traditions, ("the 12 and 12") is also used extensively by AA. Alcoholics Anonymous is now a worldwide program with 100,131 groups and 2,215,293 members worldwide. As of January, 2002 in the United States, there were 51,245 groups and 1,160,651 members.[1] Alcoholics Anonymous defines itself as follows:

> Alcoholics Anonymous is a fellowship of men and women who share their experience, strength and hope with each

other that they may solve their common problem and help others recover from alcoholism.

The only requirement for membership is a desire to stop drinking. There are no dues or fees for membership; we are self-supporting through our own contributions. A.A. is not allied with any sect, denomination, politics, organization or institution; does not wish to engage in any controversy; neither endorses nor opposes any causes. Our primary purpose is to stay sober and help other alcoholics to achieve sobriety.[2]

The goal of a member of AA is to stop drinking and never again take the first drink. The successful member is one who no longer drinks. "It is assumed that the alcoholic has a special mental and physical reaction to alcohol that renders him or her unable to resist once drinking has begun."[3]

The first three steps of the 12-step AA program follow:

1. We admitted we were powerless over alcohol—that our lives had become unmanageable.
2. Came to believe that a Power greater than ourselves could restore us to sanity.
3. Made a decision to turn our will and our lives over to the care of God *as we understood Him*.[4]

Steps Four, Five, Six and Seven call for a personal inventory, revealing this inventory to God and one other person, and being willing to have one's character defects removed by one's Higher Power. Steps Eight and Nine involve rebuilding personal relationships, making amends and restitution to others. Step Ten is a commitment to continue to take personal inventory and to make changes when necessary. Step Eleven involves improving one's personal contact with "God as we understood him." Step Twelve is a service step: to carry "this message of AA" to others. Each group of AA is autonomous. This allows AA groups to vary widely as to how they apply the twelve steps.

Alcoholics Anonymous does not identify or define "God" or this "higher power." Bill W., the co-founder, had a certain antipathy toward a personal "God." He "could go for such perceptions of God as Creative Intelligence, Universal Mind or Spirit of Nature." A friend of Bill W. suggested to him, "Why don't you choose your own conception of God?" Bill W. agreed he only had to be "willing to believe in a Power greater than" himself.[5]

Nevertheless, the word "God" frequently appears in AA literature with the suggestion that alcoholics seeking recovery through AA pray to God. Many AA meetings close by reciting the Lord's Prayer or the Serenity Prayer. The Serenity Prayer follows:

God grant me the serenity
To accept the things I cannot change,
Courage to change the things I can,
And wisdom to know the difference.

Early on, Alcoholics Anonymous developed a single minded focus, namely alcoholics and alcoholism. AA did not want to expand its program to include other addictive behavior, even addiction to drugs. Consequently, in 1953, Narcotics Anonymous (NA) was started by individuals addicted to drugs other than alcohol. Narcotics Anonymous uses the twelve steps of AA and its 12 Traditions and describes its program as follows:

Narcotics Anonymous is a program of recovery from the disease of addiction. This program is for any addict who wants to stop using drugs. In Narcotics Anonymous, we believe that we can help each other to stay clean by using simple guidelines. The Twelve Steps and Twelve Traditions of NA are our guidelines; they contain the principles on which we base our recovery.

. . . Because we believe that addicts can best help other addicts, Narcotics Anonymous has no professional counselors or therapists. Membership costs nothing. NA meetings–where addicts share their experience, strength, and hope–are usually held on a regular basis. This is one of the ways in which we support one another in recovery.[6]

Because Alcoholics Anonymous did not meet the needs of the family of alcoholics, Al-Anon was started in 1951 by Lois W., wife of Bill W., co-founder of AA, and her friend, Anne B. It is a mutual self-help group for families of alcoholics.

In 1985, the LDS 12-step Addiction Recovery Program, under the direction of LDS Family Services, was started in the Salt Lake Valley. The LDS 12-step program specifically identifies AA's " higher power" as Jesus Christ. It is through Jesus Christ and his atonement that an addict can be healed of addiction. The twelve steps of both the AA program and the LDS program are set forth below. AA's twelve steps are in light print and the twelve steps used by the LDS Addiction Recovery Program are in italics:[7]

THE TWELVE STEPS

1. We admitted we were powerless over alcohol—that our lives had become unmanageable. *Admitted that we of ourselves are powerless, nothing without God.*
2. Came to believe that a Power greater than ourselves could restore us to sanity. *Came to believe that God has all power and all wisdom and that in His strength we can do all things.*

3. Made a decision to turn our will and our lives over to the care of God as we understood Him. *Made the decision to reconcile ourselves to the will of God, offer our whole souls as an offering unto Him, and trust Him in all things together.*

4. Made a searching and fearless moral inventory of ourselves. *Made a searching and fearless written inventory of our past in order to thoroughly examine ourselves as to our pride and other weaknesses with the intent of recognizing our own carnal state and our need for Christ's Atonement.*

5. Admitted to God, to ourselves, and to another human being the exact nature of our wrongs. *Honestly shared this inventory with God and with another person, thus demonstrating the sincerity of our repentance, and our willingness to give away all our sins that we might know Him.*

6. Were entirely ready to have God remove all these defects of character. *Became humble enough to yield our hearts and our lives to Christ for His sanctification and purification, relying wholly upon His merits, acknowledging even our own best efforts as unprofitable.*

7. Humbly asked Him to remove our shortcomings. *Humbly cried unto the Lord Jesus Christ in our hearts for a remission of sins that through His mercy and His grace we might experience a mighty change of heart, lose all disposition to do evil, and thus be encircled about in the arms of safety because of His great and last sacrifice.*

8. Made a list of all persons we had harmed, and became willing to make amends to them all. *Made a list of all persons we had harmed and became*

willing to make restitution to all of them (even those we had harmed in what we might have considered righteous anger), desiring instead to be peacemakers and to do all that we could to come unto God by being first reconciled to others.

9. Made direct amends to such people wherever possible, except when to do so would injure them or others. *Made restitution directly to those we had harmed, confessing our own wrong doing in each instance except when to do so would further injure them or others.*

10. Continued to take personal inventory and when we were wrong promptly admitted it. *Realizing that the weakness to be tempted and to sin is a part of the mortal experience we continued to take personal inventory and when we were wrong promptly admitted it, being willing to repent as often as needed.*

11. Sought through prayer and meditation to improve our conscious contact with God as we understood Him, praying only for knowledge of His will for us and the power to carry that out. *Sought through prayer and meditation to improve our conscious contact with God seeking the words of Christ through the power of the Holy Ghost that they might tell us all things that we should do, praying only for a knowledge of His will for us and the power to carry that out.*

12. Having had a spiritual awakening as a result of these steps, we tried to carry this message to alcoholics, and to practice these principles in all our affairs. *Having experienced a mighty change and having awakened unto God as a result of our sincere*

repentance demonstrated in taking these steps, we were willing to become instruments in carrying this message to others and to practice these principles in all our affairs.

Most of the alcohol and drug addicts who come to the LDS 12-step meetings are very familiar with Alcoholics Anonymous and Narcotics Anonymous and their 12-step programs. Many have been through one to five or more rehabilitation facilities where the 12-step program was an integral part of the treatment regimen. Participation in AA or professional treatment based on the twelve steps of AA is the dominant approach to alcoholism treatment in the United States.[8] Addicts do not come to an LDS 12-step meeting because it is a Church meeting, held in an LDS chapel, where missionaries teach gospel principles. They come because it is recommended as a "good" 12-step meeting, and they are familiar with the format.

LDS Addiction Recovery meetings are held in LDS chapels and, in the Salt Lake Valley, in the County jail and the Utah State prison. The meetings follow the AA format. Dress is casual. Meetings in chapels are usually held in a large room where chairs are arranged in a semi- circle. At each meeting there is a pair of LDS Addiction Recovery missionaries and a facilitator. The meetings are opened and closed with prayer. At each meeting a missionary speaks five to ten minutes about the step under consideration. Then the facilitator, who is a recovering addict, "shares" his or her own personal feelings and experiences as they relate to the step under discussion and bears testimony that the twelve steps work. Those in attendance are then asked to share their feelings and experiences. Each meeting lasts one and one-half hours.

You need not be a member of the Church to attend the LDS 12-step meeting. Anyone who has an interest in overcoming the problems of addiction can attend. You need not be a full-blown addict. Relatives of addicts are also welcome to attend. Only first names are used. Confidentiality is a foundational principle of the program. Everything that is discussed or heard at the meeting stays within the four walls of the meeting place.

LDS Addiction Recovery groups, under the direction of local LDS Family Service Agencies, are presently available in Arizona, California, Colorado, Florida, Georgia, Idaho, Illinois, Nevada, New Hampshire, New Mexico, Oregon, Texas, Utah, and Washington. Approximately 88 local agencies of LDS Family Services exist in the United States and four in Canada. You can find out if there is an LDS Addiction Recovery meeting in a particular area in the United States and Canada by calling the local LDS Family Service Agency. A new Church website, www.providentliving.org, lists addresses and phone numbers of all existing local agencies.

Alcoholics and addicts are physically sick and spiritually sick. The spiritual destruction that occurs in the lives of addicts from the use of alcohol or drugs is terrible. Elder Stephen L. Richards has stated:

> Every commandment of God is spiritual in nature. . . . The Word of Wisdom is spiritual. It is true that it enjoins the use of deleterious substances and makes provision for the health of the body. But the largest measure of good derived from its observance is in increased faith and the development of more spiritual power and wisdom. Likewise, the most regrettable and damaging effects of its infractions are spiritual, also. Injury to the body may be comparatively trivial to the damage to the soul in the destruction of faith and the retardation of spiritual growth.[9]

Elder Boyd K. Packer states:

> I have come to know . . . that a fundamental purpose of the Word of Wisdom has to do with revelation. . . . If someone under the influence [of harmful substances] can hardly listen to plain talk, how can they respond to spiritual promptings that touch their most delicate feelings? As valuable as the Word of Wisdom is as a law of health, it may be much more valuable to you spiritually than it is physically.[10]

With addiction, prayer ceases, scripture reading ceases, church attendance ceases. "Street values" soon replace the values of the gospel. Lying and dishonesty become second nature to the addict. "Goodness, kindness, mercy, love, empathy, altruism, self-awareness, courage, willpower, heroism, honor, duty, truth, and simple decency . . . are twisted and torn, bruised and blooded by the disease."[11]

The addict easily falls into the cesspool of pornography and immorality. Women sell their bodies to secure money to buy drugs to support their habit. The addict often gets to the point where he or she feels there is no way back: "I have gone too far down; there is no hope for me. Heavenly Father could never forgive me."

Addicts come to the LDS meetings because they are suffering, because the pain has become too intense to bear alone, and because they no longer desire to stay in their hole of depression and loneliness. They coming to the meetings to be healed by the power of the atonement of Jesus Christ, both physically and spiritually. Many come because it is their last hope. They may have gone through four or more rehabilitation programs, but yet they are still addicted to alcohol or drugs. Jesus Christ can heal the addict both physically and spiritually. He can heal the brain and the body of the addict and cleanse the spirit.

The Savior's atonement is the focus of the LDS 12-step program: that each person can be forgiven of their sins and when they are forgiven, the Lord remembers their sins no more (D&C: 58:42).

Elder Boyd K. Packer states:

> Save for the exception of the very few who defect to perdition, there is no habit, no addiction, no rebellion, no transgression, no apostasy, no crime exempted from the promise of complete forgiveness. That is the promise of the atonement of Christ.[12]

The addict must approach the Savior with "a broken heart and a contrite spirit" and a willingness to incorporate into his life the principles of the gospel of Jesus Christ.

Elder Jeffrey Holland has stated:

> Everything in the gospel teaches us that we can change if we really want to, that we can be helped if we truly ask for it, that we can be made whole, whatever the problems of the past.[13]

Those who attend the meetings are counseled to read their scriptures every day, particularly the Book of Mormon, say their prayers twice a day, and come to as many meetings as they can. Those who are members or have been members of the Church, are counseled to attend Church and have close contact with their bishop.

Although the 12-step LDS Addiction Recovery Program involves gospel principles, it is not the "gospel," nor does it replace the programs of the Church. One of the primary purposes of the 12-step LDS Addiction Recovery Program is to help addicts who are disaffected, disfellowshiped, or excommunicated members to regain full fellowship in the Church. Some who attend meetings turned their back on the Church at a young age and "just walked away and never looked back." Many have never had testimonies or any acquaintance with the Spirit and no familiarity with the Book of Mormon.

The LDS 12-step Addiction Recovery Program is not designed to teach the "gospel" to the addict. This is not its purpose. It is not a missionary class, a gospel doctrine class, or a priesthood class. The purpose of the LDS 12-step Addiction Recovery Program is very limited. First, it is to help the addict have a spiritual awakening and receive a witness that he can recover from his or her addiction and be forgiven through the atonement of Jesus Christ, and second, it is to actively start the process of repentance, including confession to one's bishop. Once the recovering addict has this spiritual awakening and talks with his or her bishop, he or she will start participating in Church and can be taught all of the other principles and programs of the Church.

IS THE LDS 12-STEP ADDICTION RECOVERY PROGRAM ALL THAT IS NEEDED TO RECOVER?

Is the LDS 12-step program, which is authorized by the Church, all that a person needs in order to recover from addiction to alcohol or drugs? Are rehabilitation programs and therapists really necessary? Why not save your money, just attend one LDS 12-step meeting a day, pray twice a day, read the scriptures and work the steps? There are many who will tell you that they got clean and sober by only working the AA or LDS 12-step programs.

Certainly the Savior has the power to heal any mental or physical illness including that of addiction. Does this mean that additional help from professionals should not be sought? The answer is certainly no. If you have cancer or severe heart problems, no Church authority would suggest that you rely only on priesthood blessings and not consult an oncologist or heart specialist. Likewise, when one is dealing with a life threatening illness, such as addiction, professional help should be sought. The LDS 12-step program can and ought to be an integral part of any treatment program.

7

The Family—Caught in the Nightmare of Addiction

Within each addict's circle of suffering and chaos there are three or four family members—parents, a spouse and particularly children—who are severely impacted by the addiction. Addiction is a family disease. The destruction of the family by the addict takes the form of family arguments, ruined holidays, legal problems, emergency room visits, job-loss, financial ruin, arrest, incarceration, and traffic accidents with personal injury and death.

At least a fourth of the population is part of a family that is affected by an addictive disorder in a first-degree relative. The data also suggest that up to 90% of actively addicted individuals live at home with a family or significant other.[1]

The addict is consumed by his or her love of alcohol or drug of choice. He or she is totally egocentric and selfish. Family relationships are important only as they aid him or her in obtaining the next drink or fix. Trust between the addict and family members is absolutely destroyed. Addicts are liars and consummate manipulators. You cannot believe anything an addict says whether drunk or sober. You cannot have a rational conversation with an addict under the influence of alcohol or drugs. Any attempt will only lead to total frustration on the part of the family member and anger on the part of the addict. The addict may even accuse a family member as being the cause of his addiction. In the family there may be an unspoken ban on the expression of negative feelings, such as anger or resentment. Children of addicts come to learn three basic family rules: "don't feel, don't talk and don't trust."[2]

The family often lies for the addict to cover up his or her drinking or drug abuse, and the family becomes isolated as it struggles to hide the family secret. Everyone in the family is careful not to upset the addict. Family members are controlled by the addict because of the fear of an outburst of anger or verbal or physical abuse.

The addict denies that he or she has a problem or that his or her drinking or using is causing the family any problems. The family may also be in denial. The family wants to believe that the family is normal, and they suppress their feelings about the reality of the addiction. Because the family is ashamed of the addict's behavior, they seek isolation in an effort to hide the family secret.

> Typical defense mechanisms adopted by families include classic denial that there is a problem, minimization of the magnitude of the problem, projection of the problem of blame for the problem onto others, and rationalization or excusing the problem away. Through use of these mechanisms, family members attempt to protect themselves or to reinforce the normalcy and worth of their family system.[3]

Because of the LDS prohibition on drinking alcohol or using drugs, any LDS family will probably have an even more difficult time facing the reality that one of its members is an alcoholic or drug addict. For the family to admit this fact to the bishop and to ward members and friends takes a lot of courage. It is easy to say, "My son is a diabetic", but very difficult to say, "My son is an alcoholic." There is social stigma attached to one but not the other. If the family understands the disease concept of addiction, it is easier for the family to overcome their denial and seek the needed help from the members of the Church.

Family members enmeshed in the addict's life have difficulty knowing how to respond to the addict or how to help him recover from his addiction. Latter-day Saints have been taught all of their lives:

- Go the extra mile.
- Turn the other cheek.
- Love those who spitefully use you.
- Do not judge.
- Do not get resentful or angry.
- Be patient, humble, meek and longsuffering.
- Bear your afflictions gracefully.
- Think of others, not yourself.
- Care and comfort those who are sick.
- Sacrifice your time and material goods for others.

The foregoing gospel tenets are true. However, if not applied with judgment, wisdom, and great care, they can lead into the quagmire of codependency. Other gospel principles are equally true and must also be applied:

- Each person is responsible for their own salvation.
- Your first responsibility is to save yourself.
- You cannot help another person if your own spiritual and emotional reservoir is empty.
- Each person has their own moral agency which should remain inviolate.
- You should not do for others what they can do for themselves.
- A person should bear the consequences of his actions.

The true follower of Christ wants to show love and compassion toward the addict and to do everything possible to help the addict recover. Often it is difficult to determine where true Christian love and compassionate actions end and where harmful codependent enabling actions begin. Protecting the addict or meeting only his wants and needs leads to the debilitating problem of codependency.

CODEPENDENCY

The term "codependent" is derived from the fact that the codependent's feelings and behavior are dependent upon what the addict might or might not do. Codependency is being so concerned and obsessed with your addict, about how you can change or control his behavior, that you destroy your own life and opportunities for happiness. You are obsessed with the addict's wants and needs instead of your own:

> Codependency is a disease of lost selfhood, of having one's self and self-esteem defined by someone else's behavior. The codependent person is as hooked on the addict as the addict is hooked on the alcohol or other drug. Codependents neglect their own inner, deeper needs as they try tirelessly but futilely to fix themselves by fixing the addicted person in their lives. Codependent people have trouble thinking of themselves without thinking of their addicts. Their lives and self-concepts, to a large extent, are defined by their relationships with their addicts.[4]

As the codependent person suppresses his or her true desires and feelings, a false self emerges which strives to please the alcoholic. The codependent no longer develops independent opinions or interests. Rather, the goal of the codependent is the expression of opinions which will be approved by the alcoholic and to engage in behaviors which serve the interests of the alcoholic.[5]

Codependency comes in varying degrees. It is important to recognize the characteristics of a codependent and to avoid them so that they do not destroy your own well-being. The following are codependent characteristics:

- Spending exorbitant time worrying or obsessing about the addict.
- Trying to control the addict's behavior through advice, rewards, threats, coercion, guilt, manipulation or dominance.
- Always willing to sacrifice your own wants and needs for the wants and needs of the addict.
- Feeling guilty because you are not doing enough to help the addict recover.
- Feeling unappreciated for what you sacrifice, then resentful and angry because the addict has used you over and over again.
- Sacrificing all of your financial means, to the point of poverty, to pay for treatment and care of the addict.
- Willing to always rescue and protect the addict from the consequences of his addictive behavior.
- Saying "yes" when you mean "no."
- Believing that if you pray more, fast more and are more obedient to the gospel the addict will get better.
- Refusing to express your true feelings because it will make the addict drink or use more.
- Willing to accept verbal, emotional and sometimes physical abuse from the addict, believing that this time you can trust the addict and that he will do what he has promised.
- Believing that if the addict would only stop drinking or using drugs then we could start living.

- Having one's thoughts and conversations always drift towards the addict: Will he drink tonight or over the weekend? Will he lose his job, and what will happen if he loses his job?
- If the addict drives, worrying about whether or not he will kill or seriously injure himself or some innocent third person.

DETACHMENT

"We cannot begin to work on ourselves, to live our own lives, feel our own feelings and solve our own problems until we have detached from the object of our obsession."[6] If a family member is to survive the addiction of the one he loves, he must detach or release himself from the addict and his enmeshing addiction. It is done not because we do not care or love the addict. We detach because we do care, and because we must care for ourselves. Attempting to control another person's behavior is futile; no amount of control can effect a permanent change in another's behavior. Detachment is based on the key principle that: "I have to take care of myself, or I am of no use to any one else."

> Detachment is neither kind nor unkind. It does not imply judgment or condemnation of the person or situation from which we are detaching. It is simply a means that allows us to separate ourselves from the adverse effects that another person's alcoholism can have upon our lives. Detachment helps families look at their situations realistically and objectively, thereby making intelligent decisions possible.[7]

ANTIDOTES FOR CODEPENDENCY

- Do not try to control the behavior of your addict or solve his problems.

Trying to control addictive behavior is an exercise in total futility. No matter what you do, if the addict wants to drink or use, he or she will find a way to do it. Stop hiding the bottle or nagging. Do not try to reason with the addict when drunk or high. It is impossible. If the addict is in jail because of his actions, you should probably leave him there. At least he will be safe and clean for a while. Jail time can help someone in denial to seek treatment. You cannot protect the addict from the self-destruction of his or her addiction.

- Take responsibility for your own happiness.

You are responsible for your own physical, emotional, spiritual and financial well-being. Stop blaming others for your circumstances. Stop complaining or whining. You have better health and more wealth than millions of other individuals. Your glass is half full, not half empty. Whether or not you are happy or sad, is up to you.

- Love and value yourself.

You are a child of God. You are unique, one of a kind. You have a mind that is capable of an ultimate expansion. You have "great gifts, greater endowments, and the greatest of destinies" (Truman Madsen). Love yourself as the Savior loves you. Though you are the weakest of Saints, you can, through the gospel of Jesus Christ, become as He is.

- Spend time alone.

Go for a ride in the car alone. Go to the temple alone and sit quietly in the celestial room to pray, meditate and gather strength. Go for a long walk alone. Find a place to rest and to meditate. Go to the library or a bookstore alone and browse and read. Stay there as many hours as you want.

- Get rid of your resentments.

   Get rid of your resentments and anger toward your addict. Pray for the strength to completely forgive him "for he that forgiveth not his brother . . . there remaineth in him the greater sin" (D&C 64:9). Do not continue to carry this baggage around. Drop it at the feet of the Savior.

- Join an Al-Anon Group.

   Al-Anon groups are self-help support groups for family members "who share their experience, strength and hope, in order to solve their common problems." The emphasis is on helping the family member, not the addicted family member. Al-Anon meetings help the members learn to free themselves of feeling responsible for the addiction of their family member.

- Trust in God.

   Live righteously. Be obedient and then put your trust in God: "for all flesh is in mine hands; be still and know that I am God" (D&C 101:15). Things may not turn out as you hope or expect. Your addict may not recover. She may die or go to jail or prison. You didn't cause her addiction and you can't control it. It is in God's hands.

- Satisfy your own wants and needs.

   Satisfying your own wants and needs is important. Do not sacrifice them at the expense of the wants and needs of your addict. Buy that new dress or that new book. Go to the movie when you want to. Do not cancel your appointments or plans because of what the addict may want to do. Do not become a captive in your own home.

PEACE, COMFORT, AND STRENGTH AMIDST CHAOS

The disease of addiction is inscrutable. The actions of an alcohol or drug addict are without logic or rationality. In the face of immediate and disastrous consequences the addict will continue to drink or use drugs. The family of an addict becomes very confused as they try to cope with the irrational and self-destructive behavior of someone they love. They wonder if their acts of love and compassion toward the addict will only enable the addict to go deeper and deeper into his addiction. Where is the line between love and enabling? How does one apply "tough love" in face of the specter that it will almost surely subject the one they love to serious injury or death?

Family members understand that life is full of adversity, trial and affliction. But why are the cravings for alcohol or drugs miraculously taken away from some addicts while our prayers for our loved ones seem to go unanswered? Are not we as righteous and deserving as someone else? The logic and reasons for the seeming inequality of afflictions cannot be understood in this life. Only God is omniscient. As Elder Neal A. Maxwell has so aptly said, "We cannot do the sums, because we do not have all the numbers."[8] God does not expect us to solve the equation when we do not have or understand all of the relevant information.

Then what should be our course of action? We should read the Book of Mormon every day. It was written by prophets under the influence of the Spirit. As we read it, we will feel the influence of the Spirit. We must live as righteously as we can and try with all our heart to live by the Spirit, to learn how to obtain the Spirit and to discern its whisperings, and then have the faith and courage to follow its promptings. This is not easy, but it is a quest upon which we must embark. In many circumstances, as we deal with the addictive behavior of someone we love, it is only by the guidance of the Spirit that we can have any assurance that we are making the best or the correct decision.

Elder Boyd K. Packer has described the promptings of the Spirit as follows:

> We do not have the words (even the scriptures do not have the words) which perfectly describe the Spirit. The scriptures generally use the word "voice," which does not exactly fit. These delicate, refined spiritual communications are not seen with our eyes, nor heard with our ears. And even though it is described as a voice, it is a voice that one feels, more than one hears.
>
> . . . The voice of the Spirit is described in the scripture as being neither 'loud' nor 'harsh.' It is 'not a voice of thunder, neither . . . voice of a great tumultuous noise.' But rather, 'a still voice of perfect mildness, as if it had been a whisper,' and it can 'pierce even to the very soul' and 'cause [the heart] to burn.'
>
> . . . The Spirit does not get our attention by shouting or shaking us with a heavy hand. Rather it whispers. It caresses so gently that if we are preoccupied we may not feel it at all.[9]

Family members caught in the nightmare of addiction pray that their loved one will be healed of his or her addiction. They pray for years and still there is no healing. The heavens seem sealed. Occasionally you will hear a family member say, "I am now praying that if she cannot be healed, that the Lord will take her home." This is a prayer for relief from pain—the addict's and the family's. The Holy Ghost will comfort us, and the Savior will give us the strength to endure. He has gone below all things. There is no suffering, no pain, and no sorrow that He did not experience in the

Garden of Gethsemane. He did this "in order to succor his people" (Alma 7:12). As we pray fervently for comfort and strength, they will come. Of this we can be assured.

8
Prevention—
Protecting Our Children

The prevention of initial alcohol and drug use and inter-rupting the progression of substance abuse to addiction involves both education and changes in attitudes and behav-iors. When it comes to prevention there are no guarantees. The community, schools, and parents can do everything right, and some children will still have problems with addiction. Prevention is the process of reducing, not eliminating, the risk of addiction.

INFORMATIONAL APPROACH TO PREVENTION

Prior to 1980, school-based efforts to prevent alcohol and drug use were based on providing students with factual informa-tion on alcohol and drugs, drug use, pharmacological effects, and the adverse consequences of substance abuse. These educa-tional efforts were based on the underlying assumption that the problem of substance abuse was caused by inadequate knowl-edge of the danger of using alcohol and drugs. This assumption was apparently incorrect.

Evaluation studies of informational approaches to preven-tion have tended to show some impact on drug knowledge and anti-drug attitudes, but consistently have failed to show an impact on tobacco, alcohol, or drug use behavior or intentions to use drugs.[1]

SOCIAL AND PEER RESISTANCE SKILLS FOR ADOLESCENTS

Presently the primary focus of prevention of substance abuse by adolescents is teaching them skills or tactics to resist the influence that come from their peers and the media to use alcohol and drugs.

> With respect to the media, adolescents are taught how to identify and respond to pro-drug messages in advertisements, movies, rock videos and so on. Special attention is generally afforded the persuasive appeals used by advertisers to promote the sale of tobacco and alcohol products. Students are taught how to identify specific advertising techniques, to analyze ads and their messages, and to formulate counter arguments to common advertising appeals.[2]

Adolescents are taught and given training in a set of skills that they can use to resist offers from their peers to smoke, drink or use drugs:

> Prevention programs that include resistance skills training emphasize verbal and nonverbal skills for resisting these offers to use drugs. That is to say, they teach adolescents what to say when they are offered or pressured to engage in some form of drug use as well as how to say it in the most effective way possible.[3]

In the past two decades there has been a gradual accumulation of empirical studies that show that the prevention approach of social and peer resistance skills training has been effective in reducing substance abuse. For the short-term there are studies that indicate a 40% to 75% reduction in substance abuse. With respect to long-term, studies show that the effectiveness of these prevention programs erodes over time with effects being maintained for only one or two years.

D.A.R.E. (DRUG ABUSE RESISTANCE EDUCATION)

Each year about 26 million school children in the United States are taught the D.A.R.E. program which gives them the skills to avoid involvement in drugs, gangs and violence. The D.A.R.E. program is now implemented in nearly 80% of the nation's school districts. "D.A.R.E. is a police officer led series of classroom lessons that teach children from kindergarten to 12th grade how to resist peer pressure and live productive and drug and violence free lives."[4]

In the D.A.R.E. elementary program in Chesterfield, Missouri, the students are asked to write an essay about what they have learned from the D.A.R.E. program. In her essay, a delightful fifth grader, Lauren Moore, said:

> I think it is important to be drug free and violence free. You should not kill yourself by doing something that can kill you. . . . If you do drugs you will not be showing a good example for your little brother, sisters, or anybody. When you do drugs you might not get to follow your dreams.

Some of the D.A.R.E. curriculum[5] includes:
- Understanding the Effects of Mood Altering Drugs
- Considering Consequences
- Learning Resistance Techniques—Ways to Say No
- Building Self-Esteem
- Learning Assertiveness—A Response Style
- Combating Media Influences on Drug Use and Violence
- Saying Yes to Positive Alternatives
- Having Positive Role Models

RISK AND PROTECTIVE FACTORS IN DRUG PREVENTION

Over the course of more than 20 years of drug abuse research,The National Institute on Drug Abuse (NIDA), has identified important principles for use in prevention programs in the family, school, and community. Prevention programs are designed to enhance "protective factors" and to reduce "risk factors." Research has also shown that many of these same factors apply to other behaviors such as youth violence, delinquency, school dropout, risky sexual behaviors, and teen pregnancy.

Protective factors:
- strong and positive family bonds
- parental monitoring of children's activities and peers
- clear rules of conduct that are consistently enforced within the family
- involvement of parents in the lives of their children
- success in school performance; strong bonds with institutions such as school and religious organizations
- adoption of conventional norms about drug use

Risk factors:
- chaotic home environments, particularly in which parents abuse substances or suffer from mental illnesses
- ineffective parenting, especially with children with difficult temperaments or conduct disorders
- lack of parent-child attachments and nurturing
- inappropriately shy or aggressive behavior in the classroom
- failure in school performance
- poor social coping skills
- affiliations with peers displaying deviant behaviors
- perceptions of approval of drug-use behavior in family, work, school, peer, and community environments.[5]

THE ROLE OF THE FAMILY

The family, of course, plays a critical role in the prevention of substance abuse by children. While children are most at risk from substance abuse between the ages of twelve and twenty, prevention is a life-long process and begins with teaching your children the gospel and nurturing values that will protect and sustain them. Robert L. Dupont, a prior director of the National Institute on Drug Abuse, has outlined ten practical ways to "drug-proof your child."[6]

1. Set a Family Standard on Drug and Alcohol Use.

    For an LDS family, the standard is total abstinence from the use of tobacco, alcohol, and illicit drugs. Your children should know that this is the family standard. Remember that early smoking and drinking can be the gateway to the use of and addiction to marijuana, meth, cocaine or heroin.

2. Establish Reasonable Consequences For Violations of the Family Rules.

    Make the consequences for violation of family rules clear, in advance, and impose them without exception. The best punishments usually are those that are immediate and painful but fairly brief.

3. Set Aside a Time Every Day to Talk With Your Kids about What is Happening in Their Lives, How They Feel, and What They Think.

    Listen to your children, giving them your full attention. Repeat your children's experiences and feelings. Make time every day to listen to your children to let them know that you value them just the way they are, and that you want to know what they think and what they feel.

4. Help Your Children Establish Personal Goals.

Define with your children simple practical goals which could include academic, artistic and social goals. Goals should be both short-term, the next day or two, and long-term, the next month or two. Goals should be realistic.

5. Know Your Children's Friends and Spend Time With Them.

Your children's peers have a tremendous influence on their decision to use alcohol or drugs. Make sure your home is a welcome place for your children's friends. You should also know and become acquainted with the parents of your children's friends.

6. Help Your Children Feel Good About Themselves and Their Achievements, Large and Small.

Get excited about what your children do and care about. Become engaged in the activities of your children. Let your children know what is going on in your lives and know what is going on in your children's lives.

7. Have a System For Conflict Resolution.

Disagreements between parents and children are to be expected. The parents' decisions are the rules, but they should be open to appeals from their children. Establish a process for review, such as seeing a religious advisor, a mutually respected family member, a neighbor or a counselor if conflicts develop.

8. Talk About Your Children's Future Early and Often.

What do you expect from your children and what can they expect of you? Help your children understand that a good education, and college or vocational training is necessary for them to support themselves when they leave home. Show excitement about what your children want and hope to be in the future.

9. Enjoy Your Kids.

Work with your children to make your home a positive place for everyone. That means family teamwork and mutual respect.

10. Be a Nosy Parent.

Ask your children questions: know where they are and who they are with. Let your children know that you are being nosy because it is your job as their parent and because you love them.

FAMILY HOME EVENING, PRAYER, AND SCRIPTURE STUDY

Having family home evening, family prayer, and family scripture study on a consistent basis is a must. These are not optional activities. They can build a strong bond of love and trust between parents and children. They can enhance and reinforce the "protective factors" set forth in this chapter. In family home evening many of the "practical ways to drug proof your child" listed in this chapter can be discussed and implemented. Strong family relationships are necessary to offset the peer pressure on children to smoke, drink, or use drugs.

EXPRESSIONS OF LOVE BETWEEN PARENTS AND CHILDREN

Verbal and physical expressions of love are the strong cords that bind a family together. The first "protective factor" listed in this chapter is "strong and positive family bonds." Small children need to be held and hugged and spoken to softly, "I love you." Teenagers need to be hugged and hear the words, "I love you."

Frequently, in attending family sessions in rehabilitation facilities, I have heard teenagers and young adults say, "My parents never told me that they loved me," or "There were never any expressions of love in our family." One time a mother responded, "That's the way I was raised and that's the way we do it." What a tragedy for a child to be raised in a family where no love is expressed. Wise parents will shower their children with love.

INFORMATIONAL WEB SITES

The following web sites have information about alcohol and drugs and how to keep your children alcohol and drug free:

www.dare.com

> Sponsored by D.A.R.E. (Drug Abuse Resistance Education) a national non- profit organization.

www.family.samhsa.gov.

> Sponsored by the U.S. Department of Health and Human Services, Substance Abuse and Mental Health Services Administration, Center for Substance Abuse Prevention. The pamphlet "Keeping Youth Drug Free," can be downloaded from here:

www.niaa.nih.gov

> Sponsored by the National Institute on Alcohol Abuse and Alcoholism and the National Institutes of Health.

www.theantidrug.com

> Sponsored by the National Youth Anti-Drug Media Campaign. The pamphlet "Keeping Your Kids Drug-Free," can be downloaded from this web site.

9

Conclusion — There is Hope

*You can live without love,
but you cannot live without hope.*

—Elder Vaughn J. Featherstone

Some die as a result of their addiction. Some spend wasted years and decades in jail or prison. Some get clean and sober, then relapse over and over again in a seemingly unending cycle of despair.

But no matter how long and dark the night of addiction has been, there is hope—some, through the grace of God, bring their disease of addiction into remission. They remarry and enjoy the blessings of the temple. Relationships with children, parents, brothers, and sisters are restored. They buy a car and a home and enjoy the material blessings of this life. They become happy and joyful. They obtain a secure hope of a glorious resurrection.

Look around you and focus your eyes on those who have made it through the long night of loneliness and despair. You will find many of them in the LDS 12-step meetings that you attend. Many will be participants and some will be facilitators and missionaries. They will extend their hand of love and will tell you, "You can make it." Believe them, for what they say is true.

However, you cannot do it alone. Place your complete trust in God. Go to Him in mighty prayer with a broken heart and a contrite spirit. Put behind you the evils of the world. Immerse yourself in the Spirit of the Lord. Jesus Christ can heal you, and through His atonement you can be washed clean and made free.

10
Personal Stories

Even though I was born and raised in an active LDS home, and have been a very active member of the Church for the majority of my life, I became addicted to a variety of substances. Being very conscientious as to how things looked to the outward world (and in my home town, that meant the Mormon culture in our community), the majority of the substances I abused, and finally became fully addicted to, were prescription medications and food. These were acceptable after all. The prescriptions came from a doctor and a pharmacy, not from the streets. How oblivious I was to the seriousness of the drugs I was using. Prescriptions or not, they were still drugs. And as to food, well, in our culture, do I really need to explain the acceptability and availability of food?

My addictions began in my childhood. My mother abused prescriptions. And she taught me well. Started me early. By saying this, I do not mean that she was to blame for my addictions. Only that she was a model of the strung out Molly Mormon, looking "respectable." She even had me practice taking medications when around other people without drawing attention to myself. She was also a great cook and to not eat the bounties she prepared was considered an insult to her. But it has been and always will be *my* own vulnerabilities and disease that brought me into full addiction.

True to the example she set, I did the Molly Mormon routine pretty well myself. I was fully active in the Church, with responsible positions of leadership. Strung out on drugs. Prescription drugs. Did you know that one Xanax pill is equivalent in its effect on the mind and body as one serving of liquor? People would flatter me and say what a wonderful Relief Society president I was, and how much I seemed to get done, never suspecting that I was ablaze all the time. All this time, my abuses of my body and spirit with food were just as excessive. Any complaints about that were considered problems of vanity, not addiction.

I used lots of doctors and lots of pharmacies. I got so I couldn't face a day without popping pills. I couldn't even get out of bed without a "fix." The reverse was also true. If I wanted to sleep, or sit through a meeting without coming out of my skin, I needed barbiturates, narcotics, and so on. For in-between times, I managed to conveniently have the *right* symptoms to get doctors to give me a variety of pain pills and tranquilizers.

Along with the progressive obsession with and dependency on drugs, was an extreme compulsiveness with food. I have weighed 220 pounds and I have weighed 100 pounds. I have been hospitalized with anorexia. A few years later I was hospitalized with bulimia.

I had a pattern of secretive use of alcohol that was "like unto a life apart." It was something that was so secret that neither my children nor my husband knew anything about it. It wasn't something that brought pleasure, only pain and degradation.

I first came to the 12-step programs in 1977. I went to Al-Anon because I was concerned about someone close to me. I wanted the Al-Anon people to explain the alcoholic to me. This is called total denial on my part. No acceptance of what was going on in my own life. Seven years later, after more Al-Anon, some attendance at Alcoholics Anonymous and Overeaters Anonymous, I finally admitted I had a problem. I made a date with God: April 14, 1984. My supply would be gone then. It would be a weekend. I just would not get anymore amphetamines. I would rest over the weekend, and in my naiveté, I thought all would be well.

So, of course, I was surprised when I ended up in an emergency room. The doctors said that with the level of amphetamine use, let alone the other drugs, that I was using when I stopped, it was a miracle that I didn't go into convulsions. I was unable to function in my home, school, or career training for nearly a month. To this very day, I know it was by the loving grace of our Heavenly Father, and my Savior, that I survived that period of time. I have gone on to experience the recovery process since then.

The 12-step fellowships, and the 12 steps as a practical guide to living life on a spiritual basis, have brought amazing changes in my life. The 18-1/2 years since that Saturday in April have been full of ups and downs. I have had times of being more focused on sobriety, recovery and spirituality than others. But it has been a time of continual spiritual development.

In the year 2000, I became totally and permanently disabled. It has been necessary for me to make drastic life changes. Not only in adjusting to a different quality of health, but a drastically different life style as well. The Lord has been good to me and blessed me in a loving and protective way through difficult medical procedures. Nevertheless, at the beginning of the summer of 2002, I was full of despondency, anger, bitterness and self-pity. It just wasn't a pretty picture. Because of my health problems, I hadn't been able to go to 12-step meetings for quite awhile.

But as my attitude worsened, and my spiritual condition sickened, I decided to use the level of health and energy that had been restored to me to go to 12-step meetings again.

During this time, a friend who was concerned about me brought me to an LDS Substance Abuse Recovery Group. At first I was defensive. The plain and simple terms the spiritual recovery is phrased in, as used in the original 12-steps, were most precious to me. Probably because of their plainness, I didn't quite understand why the Church had chosen to rephrase those plain and simple truths. The fact that scriptural references were given to support each Step, as a divine principle from our Heavenly Father, didn't bother me. But the changing of the words did.

As is often true, when I become defensive, it means I have something to learn. So, I got a copy of the workbook, "He Did Deliver Me From Bondage," that we were encouraged to use in the LDS Recovery Groups. I made it a matter of intense study, prayer and discussion with anyone and everyone who would listen. As I went through this process, I found that there are immense differences between the standard Twelve Steps and those of the LDS Recovery Groups. And those differences have made *all* the difference to me.

First, the LDS Recovery Groups are presided over and conducted by the priesthood. There is a missionary and companion, who have been called of God to exercise the priesthood in those groups. The powers of heaven are called down for the healing of those of us in the groups. Sometimes the priesthood influence is so strong, it is almost tangible.

Second, the basis of the spiritual steps for recovery in the LDS Substance Abuse Recovery Groups is a personal relationship with our Savior, Jesus Christ. In the other 12-step programs, the basis of the spiritual program is referred to as: "God, as we understood Him." Each member is graciously given the opportunity to design a God, or Higher Power, that fits their concept of a power greater than themselves that is benevolent and loving and always there for them.

It would be hard to argue that our Savior doesn't fit that description, because He does. But faith, testimonies, scriptures and priesthood blessings directing us to our Savior, to be blessed and healed by His redemptive act of atonement, are not discussed in the original 12-step fellowships.

What a great and wonderful blessing it has been for me to be in the LDS Recovery Groups! To have the added benefit of the Priesthood and the clear focus of building, and continually strengthening, a personal, intimate relationship with my Savior, my Jesus.

I have been free of addictive use of amphetamines, narcotics and alcohol for 18-1/2 years. I have been free of bulimic behavior for 13 years. I am no longer bitter, angry, resentful or full of self-pity. My testimony and understanding of the Gospel have gone to a deeper level. Much deeper than ever before. And I am by no means done. What a tender, loving journey this life is, when it is in the company of our Lord and Savior, and with the blessings of the Priesthood. I say this in the name of Jesus Christ, Amen.

HR'S STORY

I can always remember being and living in fear. Not for my life or my safety for I grew up in a very secure and loving family. I was just afraid of everything that had to do outside of my home: people, school, assignments, activities, dinners and the list goes on and on. I also remember having no HOPE. I grew up in a very small town in northern Minnesota. It was a farming community and my dad was the town Doc. It appeared on the outside to be a Leave-It-to-Beaver type town. However, on the inside, it was filled with rampant alcoholism.

I remember the first drink that I ever took. I was nine years old and my grandparents were in town. We had a liquor cabinet downstairs that was easily accessed, even when locked. My brother and I poured three or four different liquors into a glass and drank the glass. I distinctly recall the feeling that came over me, once the gagging of the bad taste was gone. It was as if someone or something had taken away my fear, filling up the huge hole that was constantly in my stomach. I could feel it work its way into my stomach, numbing everything physically and emotionally. The "AAHHHHHH" effect. *I had found the answer.*

We grew up very Catholic so I was instilled with a fair amount of guilt at a young age. I don't think that it was necessarily the Catholicism, just my spirit telling me when things were not right. I was very conscientious, to a point of absolute perfection. This perfectionism was not forced upon me by my family, it was just part of who I was. Only A-grades were acceptable. Striking out in baseball was a tragedy. Losing in any sporting activity was devastating. Humanity and mistakes were unacceptable.

My second affair with alcohol came at age 12. I had been sober for three years (joke) and my brother had a small party at our house. My parents were away and there was plenty of beer in the house. I just sipped out of beer glasses and immediately felt the "AAHHHHHHH" once again. How could I have forgotten *the answer*? How could I have left my beloved for so long? The night ended with a case of severe dry heaves and pleading to God that I would never do this again, if only he would heal me. Again I swore off liquor, but again I remembered the feeling.

Around this same time I discovered marijuana. It gave you a buzz without the hangover! Awesome. My use of both alcohol and marijuana slowly escalated in my teenage years. I went from a weekend warrior, we always had a party somewhere, to an occasional weeknight, to every weeknight, to everyday. By the time I was off to college, I was fully enrolled in the Graduate School of Addiction.

I was the valedictorian of my high school class but never really took college very seriously. I attended a private Catholic school, St. Johns University in Minnesota. I was constantly in a haze from the first night at school. I remember the night the party escalated to pouring Johnny Walker Black down people's throats at my discretion. It was all part of some drinking party game.

My days at college were spent either drinking or smoking marijuana or finding ways to procure the substance. I can remember the feeling when the *score* happened. It meant all would be well in the world for as long as the stuff lasted. I remember feeling relieved, satisfied and hopeful that the stuff would get me through another day/week/month. At this point, I was using anything bad for me that made me feel good.

I rarely attended class and honed my business skills by hiring people to take my tests for me. These were general studies classes so it was not difficult to procure the services of some able minded person in my dorm. The irony is that I could have gotten A grades for free, doing it myself. At this point I was always looking for the path of least resistance, the wider gate, the easier road. Obviously, easier is not better.

After my first year I pulled out of school and at the beginning of the next semester stayed in South Dakota for one month to hunt. I returned for the Spring Semester and that was my last stint in college for awhile. The partying had reached epic proportions and my friends and I could no longer keep up the pace. The *hope* was again fading.

I still had the lingering fear that would drive most decisions. Fear of social situations, fear of losing, fear of not succeeding, etc. ad nauseum. My perfectionism had reached its pinnacle, leading to the only release of pressure from work: drinking and doing drugs. It also led to its natural conclusion, procrastination. If I didn't do anything, I could not fail and did not have to be perfect. If this makes sense to you, you are probably an addict.

I then decided, after several career stints with Taco Bell and Country Kitchen to move to Dallas with my brother. He was being transferred and at age 21 I was in the Big D. I began a job at a very exclusive Dallas hotel as the graveyard bellman. Great job in that it allowed me to smoke marijuana, unimpeded, all night long. I worked my way up the hotel corporate ladder the next few years and became the Guest Service Manager. I was always easily offended by my superiors at work. Although I was a model employee, they rarely did anything to my satisfaction and I could not deal with the denial of a promotion. It eventually led to my leaving three very good jobs in about seven years. A classic narcissist.

My drinking and use of marijuana increased during this time. I always, always, had to have something to numb my pain, to enable me to get out of reality if only for an hour each night. Many of my days were spent buying or arranging to buy my medicine. In retrospect, I probably spent five to six hours per day in my habit, either using or in the procuring.

Around the age of 26 I met a young lady at a hotel where I was working. We became immediately physically intimate and this led to our falling in love. During my courtship and eventual marriage, the use of marijuana was not permitted. Although I was caught several times, I was fairly honest for the first year. It would result in many promises being broken and a trail of concealment a mile long. I would try to get them out of the house so I could use. I would make innumerable excuses so I could leave alone and use. The list goes on and on.

Around our second year of marriage I began with a start up finance company. The company grew and went public and I moved my way through the ranks very quickly, eventually becoming their VP of National Marketing and Sales. I was the sixth employee and we ended up with 300+ employees after two years. We were riding high and I was hiring some pretty big hitters, both in sales and in drinking and using. We would hold many of our sales meetings in bars and my days consisted of around 12-14 hours.

I would start the day with a Vicodin in the morning and smoke a joint on my way to work. I was always the first one in at 6:00 a.m. so I had ample time to enjoy the "buzz." I would then take another Vicodin around 10:00 a.m., smoke another joint around noon and sometimes have a martini lunch. I spent most nights in the bar for "sales meetings." I can remember wanting to live up to my word and get home on time. The minute that I would start to drink, I would lose control of time and myself. I would look up and it would be 10:00 p.m. It was frustrating to my wife and me; however, I was making pretty big money at 30 and neither of us ever really addressed the problem.

After another grandiose business idea, I left this job and started up a business for my wife. I was going to oversee it and be "El Presidente" because no one else could do it the way that I could. My days were spent golfing and letting her find her way through the business. Obviously, this was a formula for disaster. My drinking and drug use increased at this point. I was constantly concealing my activity from my wife and child. Living a complete lie in many ways. It tugged at my spirit; however, my spirit was slowly being numbed into submission. It had been many years since I had gone to church, other than an obligatory Christmas mass with my family of origin. God was nowhere to be found in my life as there was already a god, Me. What a scary and lonely way to live one's life, self-propelled. I believe that C.S. Lewis describes that as being hell, all by oneself. I believe that to be true. The HOPE was again gone.

As you may imagine, by year four, I was ready to be on my own. My wife and I separated and eventually divorced. I lost about 30 pounds and moved to Sioux Falls to recharge my batteries. I had come to the conclusion that marijuana was my nemesis so I swore off "dope" forever. You can only guess what happened, my drinking increased dramatically. I again procured a good job and within six months was the Sales Manager. I saved up my money, was held back on a promotion to Vice President and some stock and summarily quit because of my black-and-white integrity. That'll show them.

I spent the next six months in a bottle. I spent many days alone at our hunting cabin. I'm not stupid, I always quit jobs around hunting season. My drinking increased to about one-and-a-half quarts of really bad vodka every day. My liver was expanding exponentially, and I was rarely eating a good meal. I was trying to kill myself but couldn't get myself to pull the trigger. Drinking myself to death seemed a suitable alternative. I was tired of the pain and fear and anger. I was tired of all of the "imbeciles" of the world that did me wrong. I was mad at God for giving me this lot in life. I felt more hopeless at this point than any other time in my life.

Then something happened. I woke up one morning and couldn't do it any longer. I just remember getting on my knees and asking for help. In fact, it was the only word that I used in the prayer, *HELP*. I didn't see any white lights or feel anything in particular. I just knew that it would be OK and that I wouldn't drink that day. Keep in mind, I had tried to quit hundreds of times, swearing each time that it was the last. Drinking and smoking up the remains only to wake up in a panic and looking to score by 9:00 a.m.

This time was different. There were not foxhole prayers, it was not premeditated, it just happened. It was probably the purest prayer that I had ever uttered. I know that the Lord knew my heart and His Grace poured down over me that morning. I have never wanted to drink or drug since that morning. It was March 30, 1997. I remember my Mom called that morning and asked when I would be over for dinner. I inquired as to the event. She said, "Well, it's Easter of course." I put the phone down and began to cry tears of gratitude and joy. I felt a surge of hope again in my life.

I began going to the meetings of Alcoholics Anonymous within the week. I embraced the twelve steps and did everything that my sponsor asked of me. I couldn't get enough of the spirit in those rooms. Here were people that were different in many ways, religious, social, economic, race etc., yet, there was a common bond between each other. We were all trying to survive and to live productive and joyous lives. AA taught me how to be spiritual again in my life. It showed me how to connect with Heavenly Father, to surrender to his will on a daily basis and to serve others along the way. Once the spirituality came, I longed for more knowledge, which took me back to the religion of my youth, Catholicism. As usual, I went in with guns blazing. I was the Director of the Catholic Family Sharing Appeal, which raised money for the

Diocese of South Dakota. It was very rewarding and my life seemed to be on track.

I remember an AA conference where a Catholic priest was a featured speaker. He came up to me after the conference and we decided to have breakfast together. He was a wise man and several times he leaned across the table and said "You have the aura, Brown, you are responsible for that." It hit me to the very depths of my soul. I thought that I knew what he meant, I was supposed to be a priest. I spoke about this with my Catholic bishop and of course, he concurred. I then called my brother in Salt Lake City and told him of my revelation. He said he knew that I was to be a priest. I would later find out what that meant.

My brothers asked me to come to Salt Lake City for the summer, possibly to move there. I was tentatively planning on going to the Catholic seminary in the fall. As I began to meet their friends in a singles LDS ward, I was attracted by their peaceful demeanor, similar to seeing a positive attribute in a person that you wish that you had. During this same time, I was studying the Catechism of the Catholic Church. There were some inconsistencies that didn't fit with my mind and spirit.

I began to take the LDS missionary discussions and also began to read the Book of Mormon. I focused on Moroni 10:3-5 before and after each reading. It was clear, concise and full of light and truth. The discussions were answering many of the questions that plagued my mind. They turned into quite the event with 10-12 people at a time.

The main problem was that I was still smoking two to three packs of Camels on a daily basis. I knew that I had to quit to be baptized and really felt I needed to quit more to find out if this were true or not. I went up to Lake Mary in Brighton for two days to fast and to finish the Book of

Mormon once and for all. I packed some water, tent, sleeping bag and off I went. There was one problem, when I arrived at the trailhead, I only had two cigarettes left in my pack. Here was the true test. I implored the Lord that I really, really needed his His Grace on this one. If he wanted me to join His Church, he was going to have to work some miracles with the smokes. As the saying goes, be careful of what you pray for, you just may get it and I did.

Several weeks later, after I finished the Book of Mormon, I was baptized. I can't say that I had a testimony of Joseph Smith at that time, I just knew that he did not write that book. I knew that it came from the hand of God. It was the purest text that I had ever read. The words seemed to apply to me and were understandable almost immediately.

Since then, my life has never been the same. I have a different understanding of sobriety through the gospel of Jesus Christ via The Church of Jesus Christ of Latter-day Saints. It clarifies the twelve steps for me and my "higher power" is now Jesus Christ. It assists me in my everyday efforts and is the roadmap by which I try to live my life. I can testify to all that the Book of Mormon contains the words and mind of our Heavenly Father. I would also like to testify that *I KNOW* it contains the restored gospel of Jesus Christ, with all of the proper ordinances contained within, and that our Savior sacrificed all that he had for each of us, individually. Most of all, I would like to testify that it gives me hope for this life and the life to come.

ROD'S STORY

I am Rod, a recovering addict and a very grateful son of God. I was born in Salt Lake City, Utah, of goodly parents. I was born under the covenant and with all the blessings of being born in America. I started my life with everything going for me. I remember as a child I was very insecure, but I was surrounded by a loving, caring family. I was taught gospel principles and was baptized when I was eight. I have always wanted to be a good person.

My first introduction to narcotics was at the age of 13 when I was hospitalized for an appendectomy. I still remember the euphoria that I felt. I said to my mother, "Mom, I feel like I am floating on the ceiling." I didn't realize that was the beginning of my addiction to narcotics and no one else realized it either.

My next encounter with drugs was when about 16 years old. A friend gave me some yellow pills he had taken from his grandmother. They were barbiturates called "yellow jackets." I liked the euphoria that I felt again, and it never occurred to me that it could lead me into addiction.

I was still insecure and I was becoming rebellious and trying to fit in with my friends. I started drinking with them in high school. I knew that liquor and smoking were bad and against the Word of Wisdom so I stopped doing that stupid high school stuff.

While I was in high school I sustained serious neck injuries as a result of a motorcycle accident. I started having severe headaches and, of course, the medical doctors prescribed pain pills. They prescribed Tylenol with codeine. These relieved my head aches and I thought they were miracle drugs because they also helped my insecurity.

When I was 24 I cut off half a finger in another motorcycle accident. At this time the doctor prescribed Percocet in large quantities. This prescription drug eased the pain. I felt that I had found a cure to all of my problems. However, I continued to have severe migraine headaches. I found a doctor that prescribed Fiorinal, which was a combination of codeine and barbiturates. This seemed to really fix all of my feelings and problems. In retrospect, I can see that it was covering up every feeling and problem I was having. I didn't realize I had a problem because I was getting the prescription drugs from doctors. I was not buying pills on the street like a drug addict, which meant that I couldn't be an addict. This doctor was a real "pill pusher." I could get a prescription for 50 to 100 pills and by using numerous pharmacies I could get about 2000 pills off of one prescription. As the pain got worse I increased the number of pills. It was hard for me to believe that a body could withstand 30 pills of Fiorinal a day. I am grateful to my Heavenly Father to still be alive. My "pill pushing" doctor finally cut off my supply. I think he got scared because of all the pills that I was getting from his prescriptions. I then found other doctors throughout the Salt Lake Valley where I could get my supply of Fiorinal. I would go from one doctor to another. All I had do to was to tell the doctor that I bad migraine headaches and he would write me out a prescription. Sometimes the doctor would only put one refill on the prescription. It was easy to change the "1" refill to "10" refills and more.

Notwithstanding all the pills I was taking, I didn't think I had a real problem. I was still in denial. My life was spinning hopelessly out of control, and I was becoming a wreck. Oh, the pain and anguish I brought on myself and those around me. I was becoming spiritually bankrupt. How could it be otherwise; the Spirit of the Lord does not dwell in unholy places. My drug addiction led me into indescribable despair. At this time I was doing things that were not pleasing in the eyes of God. I felt and was spiritually bankrupt. When the Holy Ghost is offended by our transgressions it withdraws from us.

I finally realized I had a real problem. My life was totally out of control. I couldn't work. I couldn't think. My life was consumed with getting more pills. Sometime in 1984 I finally checked myself into Highland Ridge Hospital for detox and treatment. I stayed there for 40 days. The first few days of detox I didn't know where I was or who I was.

After I got out of Highland Ridge, I did a 90 in 90, 90 AA meetings in 90 days. I then had a short relapse. I had gotten divorced and was now remarried. I remained clean for about seven and one-half years.

I eventually had to have radical stomach surgery. They removed two-thirds of my stomach and 15 feet of intestines. I believe that all the pills I had taken was a big cause of all the stomach ulcers that had scarred over. At the time of the operation I told the doctors that I was a drug addict. They assured me that they would only give me the morphine that was necessary to control the pain and not to worry.

I was in and out of the hospital for two months. When I got out I thought to myself, "You really handled that morphine well, I know I can control the number of Fiorinal pills, only three or four a day." I got a Fiorinal prescription and within a period of a few months I was back to using the same number of pills as in the past. So much for control.

I continued on for some time with the same number of pills and then I got arrested for prescription fraud. I had gone into a pharmacy to get a prescription filled. I was really messed up. I really needed some more pills. The pharmacist kept telling me two or three times that my prescription was not quite ready. I knew something was wrong, but I waited around. I really needed those pills. The next thing I knew I was being arrested by two cops. I pled guilty to a felony charge and the judge put me on two years probation.

After this felony conviction I only got a few prescription drugs through doctors. The arrest and conviction had frightened me. I was doing contracting work at the time, and I was in and out of people's homes. I would take drugs from their homes where I could. I was also drinking. I was attending about one AA meeting a week but not taking my recovery seriously. I was angry, resentful, and miserable.

This period of drifting through some prescription drugs, alcohol and AA meetings continued for years until a friend of mine invited me to go with him to an LDS 12-step meeting. I went a number of times. I felt something different, something good. I now realize that this was the Spirit of the Lord. However, I continued to abuse prescription drugs and then I started to drink more heavily. The more alcohol I drank the faster the adversary took me down. My new wife of about ten years who I loved dearly was thinking again of leaving me. She felt I was going to die. I was living in our rental unit that we owned. It was here that I remember feeling completely hopeless, and I realized that if I continued on the path I was on, I was going to die. I had not been active in the Church for many years, but I knew there was a God, and I knew that I had to have a priesthood blessing; I desired with all of my heart to have a priesthood blessing. I had been given blessings before but primarily because someone else had suggested it, not because I really desired it way down deep. In the morning, my parents came and took me to their home. I phoned a close relative and asked him if he would come and give me a priesthood blessing. After this priesthood blessing the cravings for drugs and alcohol left me completely. I still have thoughts and dreams about drugs and drinking, but the cravings are gone.

I started attending LDS 12-step meetings regularly. My life has changed; I have become spiritually connected with my Heavenly Father and my Savior, Jesus Christ. The emptiness and hollowness in my soul has, through obedience, begun to heal. Spiritual healing is happening in my life on a day-to-day basis. The words, "My heart has turned to you completely," are the words that my Father in Heaven had wanted so badly to hear from me for a such a long time.

I was inactive for the many years of my addiction. During this time I was led away from the gifts of our Heavenly Father by no fault but my own. Through adversity and trials I lived with a hollowness in my soul, struggling to be the good person I always wanted to be, but being drawn into the worldly ways of the adversary. By letting go of my pride, I have turned my will over to my Father in Heaven. He knows my needs much better than I.

Most of my life was in addiction until I turned my will and my life over to the care of my Savior, Jesus Christ. I lived in that roller coaster ride of addiction. There comes a time in our lives (when we have reached bottom) when a definite decision must be made. Without obedience to God's commandments our personal progression and salvation is jeopardized. If our personal progress, on a day-to-day basis, is centered in Jesus Christ, nothing can go permanently wrong. I am so grateful to be able to say that there is hope that through Jesus Christ we can change. We all have the opportunity to petition the Lord with sincerity of heart for his help in our lives. And He will answer our every prayer.

I am grateful for the LDS 12-step program that led me back to the Savior and His Church. I bear testimony to you that my prayers have been answered, and a new countenance has come over me, following the priesthood blessing that I, myself, sincerely had asked for over three years ago. I have had that change of heart. Our Father in Heaven knows each of us very well; he knows our needs better than we ourselves know. I bear testimony of the truthfulness of Joseph

Smith and the Book of Mormon, and how this book can help guide our lives. I bear testimony of the truthfulness of Jesus Christ, our Prophet and his counselors. I am grateful that they are inspired of God to give us guidance and leadership. By the grace and mercy of my Father in Heaven, may I always have these attitudes with me. May I be humble day by day, that I may be teachable, is my prayer. I say this in the name of Jesus Christ, amen.

RICK'S STORY

I grew up on a farm in Northern Utah. It was five miles from a town of 1200 people. We had few neighbors. The whole family worked from sun-up to sundown every day of the week. We had 80 head of milk cows and 300 acres of wheat and alfalfa. There were six children in the family. We went into town for church every Sunday. On Friday and Saturday nights, Mom and Dad always went to the Bloody Bucket in Idaho to drink and dance.

When I was twelve the family moved to Salt Lake City. While on the farm, Dad also worked nights for the railroad, sorting and delivering mail. He was offered a substantial pay increase if he would move to Salt Lake City. I got a job at the elementary school as a janitor for $1.35 per hour. I worked one hour before school and two hours after school. I kept this job for three years, then I got a job at a local hotel/restaurant as a busboy. I was in high school now and maintaining about a B+ average.

Throughout this whole time I attended all my church meetings regularly, paid my tithing, received my Duty To God Award, and was ordained a deacon, teacher, and priest in the Aaronic Priesthood. I fell a few merit badges short of becoming an Eagle Scout. My oldest brother was serving in the military in Germany and my second-oldest brother was serving a LDS mission in London.

In my senior year of high school I began to hang around with a group of guys whom I considered to be quite exotic and macho. I knew they drank and smoked, but I didn't believe that by associating with them I would drink or smoke. Well, of course I was wrong.

One night my buddy Wayne and I went driving around in his car. We stopped at a small grocery store and bought a six-pack of beer. He handed me a beer. I remember I didn't really want it and wasn't quite sure how to say "no" without sounding like a sissy. So I pulled the tab on top and it sprayed me up and down with beer foam. Now, at the time, I didn't have enough experience to know that if you spilled beer all over you and drank two or three of them, you would smell like a brewery. Mom would bring that to my attention later in the evening.

It had already been a full evening for me and by far one of the most exciting and eventful of my life, but I wasn't done yet. When I got home, I wished I hadn't. I quietly opened the back door of our dark house and stepped in, softly closing the door behind me. I turned to go down the stairs to my room when I was suddenly hit smack in the face by a freight train. The train backed up and hit me again. Harder this time. When my head kind of cleared and I could see again, I found out it wasn't a freight train, but dear old Mom. She followed me downstairs and into my bedroom hitting and cursing at me every chance she got.

After a while everything died down and I got to sleep. But it started up again. She came down and lit into me again. Finally, while she was catching her breath, I asked her how she dared to treat me like this when she got drunk nearly every day of her life, including the times she was in the Relief Society or Primary presidencies. That did it. I was the unfortunate soul who had dared to ask her to justify her behavior and why she would judge herself differently than me.

A few weeks later when I came home late after having had a few beers it was déjà vu all over again. The only difference this time was that I had tried pot for the first time. When I foolishly advised Mom of this fact she went completely out of control. Bless my dear mother's soul, her life was also out of control and little did I know I had just taken the wrong fork in the road. A long road.

This is when I decided to move out. I met three new friends. We spent many days and nights in clubs drinking and smoking. By now I was a full-fledged alcoholic. Almost every morning for the next 15 years I woke up with a hangover. During those 15 years I smoked pot frequently and used cocaine occasionally.

When I was twenty years old I moved into a nice two-bedroom apartment. I frequently had parties with people coming and going all day long. Once, my roommate Doug and I had a drinking contest in which he drank 27 quarts of beer before he threw up. I drank 28 and didn't throw up. "I won!" I thought.

My dear mother died from cirrhosis of the liver in 1975. My second oldest brother that served in the London Mission became gay. He died of AIDS in 1982. My mother was 47, three years younger than I am now. What a wonderful mother she was—except for the alcohol.

On Memorial Day, 1975, I got in a bad accident while riding my motorcycle and my lower left leg was severely crushed. It took 17 major surgeries before I could walk on it three years later. The one bright spot of the accident was that Vocational Rehabilitation offered to send me to college to learn a profession which would allow me to sit most of the day since I was now permanently disabled. I chose accounting. College was tough for me because I was on crutches most of the time. You had to maintain a 3.75 average to stay in the College of Business. I only had one quarter to finish when my oldest brother called me from San Antonio to work for a computer company. I wanted to finish school, but he needed me and agreed to pay me $5000.00 a month.

I lived in San Antonio for five years. With my brother and an investor we started another computer company which became successful beyond our optimistic business projections. The only thing more successful was my addiction to alcohol. My salary was exorbitant and I was drunk every workday from noon until midnight and every weekend. I had pretty much graduated from beer and now specialized in single-malt scotches and expensive wine. Lots of it. I still smoked pot occasionally and cocaine maybe once a month. I was also bored out of my gourd.

I left the computer company and took a job selling advertising signs. I stayed drunk most of the time and lived in expensive hotels all around the southwest. In spite of my drunkenness, I was soon Vice-President of Southwest Operations, earning a quarter million dollars a year. I was flying to a different city every other day conducting hiring and sales-training seminars. And I was as lonesome as could be. I missed Utah, the mountains, and my family.

I came back to Utah after living in Texas for three years. I got into the car business and still had a hangover every day. I started to use cocaine on a more regular basis. I also started to collect DUIs quite regularly. After two DUIs and one reckless, alcohol related accident, I decided to quit drinking. I also decided to start doing a lot more cocaine. A lot more cocaine. Too much to allow me to keep working.

My addiction was beyond my control and very expensive. My savings were soon gone. My retirement plans were cashed in at a 27% penalty for early withdrawal. My life insurance was cashed out. Over $300,000 wasted in the space of two or three years. Soon all the money was gone but my addiction stayed. Boy, did it stay. I pawned anything of value until I didn't have anything of value, until I didn't have a place to live. I worked day jobs to support my habit. I stole to support my habit. I did whatever I had to. I was more miserable than you can imagine. I lived in a rat- and roach-infested warehouse for three years. No hot water, no heat, cement floors, no appliances, no bathroom. Imagine taking a sponge bath when it is twenty degrees or colder. Imagine having to walk several blocks to use the restroom. I am 5'9" and weighed only 125 pounds. I would go to the homeless shelter for soup and bread three or four times a week. I wished that I were dead.

I got kicked out of the warehouse. I slept on the street and in crack-houses. Welcome if you have drugs or money— see ya if you don't. Wonderful life.

I was arrested as I pulled into a liquor store to get a bottle of rum for a girl who had failed to mention that earlier in the day her truck was used in a motel robbery and a high-speed chase. I was charged with possession of a controlled substance and paraphernalia. It was the same charge for which I had had a no-bail warrant issued against me two years earlier for failing to appear on those charges.

I knew I needed a prior conviction to be eligible for drug court and that was my rationale for not answering to the first charges which carried a sentence of one to five years in prison. Now, with two identical charges, I could serve up to ten years in prison if I was not accepted into drug court.

The first week in jail I noticed a few of the inmates on

our block going into a room about 6:30 p.m. at night. I found out it was an LDS Substance Abuse Recovery meeting. Since I didn't have anywhere else to go, I went. I don't remember the name of the missionaries at the first meeting. It may very well have been the author of this book. I do know that for the first time in 30 years I felt the spirit of God. I felt as if I were being spoken to by people who really did care about me and maybe even loved me. People really caring and loving was something I hadn't experienced for many, many years. The missionary said if we would do three things we could lick our addictions. I thought well, yeah, I could probably do three things, dying to know what they were. Of course it was to attend these meetings, read the scriptures, and pray morning and night.

I went through a year of drug court and successfully completed it, all the while doing those three simple things. I have been clean and sober about 20 months now. I have repented repeatedly and will continue to do so every day. I go to church every Sunday and an LDS Substance Abuse Recovery meeting every Thursday.

Is my life perfect now? No. I suffer from severe clinical depression and am taking several different medications to correct it. I haven't found one that works yet, but I am confident that I will. What I do have is the knowledge that my Father in Heaven loves me and that through the sacrifice of His Only Begotten Son I am able to be forgiven for all the sins I have done over the past 30 years.

I really took the scenic route during my addiction, covering all the hills and valleys and everything in between. Now I am kind of back where I started, and all the spoils of my wars have turned to dust. All I have to show for the past 30 years is the knowledge and wisdom I have learned about addiction and addicts.

The LDS Substance Abuse Recovery Program is truly a gift from God. Only three percent of crack cocaine addicts ever "recover." The rest end up dead or in prison. I consider this first 20 months of my recovery to be the greatest gift I have ever received. I cherish it and realize I only need to do three simple things to maintain it.

End Notes

INTRODUCTION

1. Howard Clinebell, *Understanding and Counseling Persons With Alcohol, Drug and Behavioral Addictions* (Abindon Press, Nashville, TN, 1998) dedication page.

2. Substance Abuse and Mental Health Services Administration, "Substance Dependence, Abuse, and Treatment." Retrieved November 24, 2003 from www.samhsa.govoas/nhsda/.

3. Allan W. Graham, M.D. and Terry K. Schultz, M.D., eds., *Principles of Addiction Medicine*, 3rd ed. (American Society of Addiction Medicine, Inc., Chevy Chase, MD, 2003), 396.

4. Utah State Division of Substance Abuse and Mental Health (2002 Annual Report), 25.

5. Jerry D. Spangler and James Thalman, "Forces of Habit; Addiction Tough to Beat" (*Deseret News*, March 24, 2002).

6. Dennis Romboy, "Heroin Silent Scourge of Sheltered Springville" (*Deseret News*, June 9, 2003).

7 "Kids are Victims in Drug Families" (*Deseret News*, March 28, 2003).

CHAPTER ONE

1. Gordon B. Hinckley, "Four "Bs for Boys" (*Ensign*, November, 1981), 40-41.

2. www.providentliving.org/ses/emotionalhealth/ (April 18, 2003).

3. Howard Clinebell, *Understanding Counseling Persons With Alcohol, Drug and Behavioral Addictions* (Abingdon Press, Nashville, TN, 1998), 10.
4. *Journal of the American Medical Association* (November 8, 1972), 1012-13.
5. The Church of Jesus Christ of Latter-day Saints, Resource Manual for Helping Families With Alcohol Problems (1984), 125.
6. Allan W. Graham, M.D. and Terry K. Schultz, M.D., eds., *Principles of Addiction Medicine,* 3rd ed. (American Society of Addiction Medicine, Inc., Chevy Chase, MD, 2003), 36.
7. Ibid., 1500.
8. Ibid., 1499.
9. Alan I. Leshner, "We Can Conquer Drug Addiction" (The Futurist, November, 1999), 22-23.
10. Allan W. Graham, M.D. and Terry K. Schultz, M.D., eds., *Principles of Addiction Medicine*, 3rd ed., 48.
11. Jerome D. Levin, Primer for Treating Substance Abusers, (Northvale, NJ, J. Aronson, 1999), 209-10.
12. Robert L. Dupont, The Selfish Brain (Hazelden, Center City, MN, 2000), 133, 135-36.
13. Alan I. Leshner, "Drug Addiction Is a Brain Disease and Should Be Treated As Such", (Science and Technology, Spring, 2001).

CHAPTER TWO

1. Robert L Dupont, *The Selfish Brain* (Hazelden, Center City, MN, 2002), 125.
2. Ibid., 147.
3. Ibid., 162.
4. Ibid., 157-58.
5. David Emmett and Graeme Nice, *Understanding Drugs* (Kingsley Publishers, London, PA, 1999), 81.

6. "Facts About Drugs: Ecstasy",Retrieved February 26, 2004 from www.safety1st.org/educate/drug-facts/ecstacy

7. "Ecstasy Fact Sheet," Retrieved March 1, 2004 from www.whitehousedrugpolicy.gov/publications/fact-sht/mdma

8. "Ecstasy", Retrieved March 1, 2004 from www.gdcada.org/statistics/ecstasy.html

9. Rod Colvin, *Prescription Drug Addiction, The Hidden Epidemic* (Omaha, NE, Addicus Books, 2002).

10. Ibid, 14.

11. "CNS Depressants", Retrieved September 11, 2002 from www.hsda.state.ut.us/prescription_htm.

12. Rod Colvin, *Prescription Drug Addiction, The Hidden Epidemic*, 20.

13. Jerome D. Levin, *Primer for Treating Drug Abusers* (Northvale, NJ, J. Aronson, 1999), 166.

14 Robert L. Dupont, *The Selfish Brain*, 220-22.

15. Ibid., 222.

16. Ibid., 230.

17. Ibid., 233.

18. Boyd K. Packer, (Conference Report, October, 1969), 36.

CHAPTER THREE

1. Howard Clinebell, *Understanding and Counseling Persons With Alcohol, Drug and Behavioral Addictions* (Abingdon Press, Nashville, TN, 1998), 47.

2. Jacob Santini, "New Hot Line Aimed at Reducing Drug Overdose Drugs" (Salt Lake Tribune, April 26, 2002).

3. Utah Division of Substance Abuse and Mental Health (2002 Annual Report), 48.

4. Joseph A. Califano, Jr., "A New Prescription" (Washington Monthly, October, 1998), 9.
5. Ibid., 9.
6. Allan W. Graham, M.D. and Terry K. Schultz, M.D., eds., Principles of Addiction Medicine, 3rd ed. (American Society of Addiction Medicine, Inc., Chevy Chase, MD, 2003), 543.

CHAPTER FOUR

1. *Matthew Cowley Speaks* (Deseret Book Co., Salt Lake City, UT, 1954), 218.
2. Ibid., 155.
3. *Teachings of the Prophet Joseph Smith*, ed. Joseph Fielding Smith (Deseret News Press, Salt Lake City, UT, 1942), 241.
4. *Shorthand Notes of Marian J. Baker, Talk of Gordon B. Hinckley*, (Regional Conference, September, 2002).
5. Phil S., *The Perfect Brightness of Hope* (Maasai, Inc., Provo, UT, 2002) 192.
6. Dallin H. Oaks, "The Laborers" (Ensign, November, 2000), 34.
7. Jerry D. Spangler and James Thalman, "Forces of Habit: Addiction Tough to Beat" (Deseret News, March 24, 2002).
8. Utah Division of Substance Abuse and Mental Health, Community Treatment Services (FY 2002 Fact Sheet).
9. American Probation and Parole Association, "Substance Abuse Treatment" (retrieved January 20, 2004 from <http://www.appa-net,org).
10. Diana H. Fishbein and Susan E. Peace, *Dynamics of Drug Abuse* (Simon & Schuster, Needham Heights, MA, 1996), 244.

11. "Salvation Army to Close Treatment Facility", (Deseret News, September 23, 2002).

CHAPTER FIVE

1. Jerome Levin, *Primer for Treating Substance Abusers* (Northvale, NJ, J. Aronson, 1999), 214-15.
2. Diana H. Fishbein and Susan E. Peace, Dynamics of Drug Abuse (Simon & Schuster, Needham Heights, MA, 1996), 10, 243.
3. "Treatment of Alcoholism - Part II", Harvard Mental Health Letter, Lester Grinspoon, M.D., ed., (June, 2000), 1-2.
4. Crescent Life, "Dual Diagnosis", Retrieved August 17, 2003 from <http://ww"w.crescentline.com/disorder/dualdiagnosis,
5. NAMI, "Dual Diagnosis: Mental Illness and Substance Abuse", Retrieved August 17, 2003 from <http://www.nami.org/helpline/dualdiagnosis.
6. "Treatment of Alcoholism - Part I", Harvard Mental Health Letter, Lester Grinspoon, M.D., ed., (May, 2000), 2.
7. National Counsel on Alcoholism and Drug Dependence, "Alcoholism and Alcohol Related Problems", Retrieved March 16, 2003 from <http://www.ncadd.org/facts/problems.
8. Allan W. Graham, M.D. and Terry K. Schultz, M.D., eds., *Principles of Addiction Medicine*, 3rd ed. (American Society of Addiction Medicine, Inc., Chevy Chase, MD, 2003), 752.
9. Janet Firshein, "Moyer On Addiction, Relapse and Craving", Retrieved January 26, 2003 from <http://www.thirteen.org/closetohome/science/html/relapsehtm.
10. Allan W. Graham, M.D. and Terry K. Schultz, M.D.,

eds., *Principles of Addiction Medicine*, 3rd ed., 827.

11. Robert L Dupont, The Selfish Brain (Hazelden, Center City, Mn, 2002), 334.

12. Katherine Ketcham and William F. Asbury, *Beyond the Influence, Understanding and Defeating Alcoholism* (Bantam Books, New York City, NY, 2000), 165.

13. Malissa Boase, "Salt Lake County Drug Court" (University of Utah Addiction Research & Education Center Newsletter), 2.

14. Division of Substance Abuse and Mental Health (2002 Annual Report), 51.

15. Alan A. Leshner, "Drug Addiction Is a Brain Disease and Should Be Treated As Such" (Science and Technology, Spring, 2001).

16. Malissa Boase, "Salt Lake County Drug Court" (University of Utah Addiction Research & Education Newsletter), 2.

17. Jerry D. Spangler and James Thalman, "Recovery From Addiction Can Be a Tough Climb", (Deseret News, March 27, 2002).

CHAPTER SIX

1. "Membership", Retrieved March 12, 2003 from www.alcoholics_anonymous.com/english/E_Fact/.

2. Id.

3. Meyer D. Glantz and Cristine R. Hartel, eds., *Drug Abuse, Origins and Interventions* (American Psychological Associates, Washington D.C., 1999), 128.

4. *Alcoholics Anonymous*, 3rd ed. (Alcoholics Anonymous World Series, Inc., New York City, N.Y., 1976), 59.

5. Ibid., 12.

6. The Twelve Steps as used by LDS Family Services Addiction Recovery Program were originally created by Heart to Heart, an LDS-oriented 12-step support group.
7. "For Those in Treatment" (Narcotics Anonymous World Series, Inc.). 1.
8. U. S. Department of Human Services, Tenth Special Report to Congress on Alcohol and Health (June, 2000), 445.
9. Stephen L. Richards (Conference Report, April, 1949), 141.
10. Boyd K. Packer, "Word of Wisdom, A Principle With Promise" (Ensign, November, 1979), 28-29.
11. Katherine Ketcham and William F. Asbury, *Beyond the Influence, Understanding and Defeating Alcoholism* (Bantam Books, New York City, NY, 2000), 191.
12. Boyd K. Packer, "The Brilliant Morning of Forgiveness" (Ensign, November, 1995), 20.
13. Jeffrey Holland, "Teaching, Preaching and Healing" (Ensign, January, 2003), 42.

CHAPTER SEVEN

1. Allan W. Graham, M.D. and Terry K. Schultz, M.D., eds., *Principles of Addiction Medicine*, 3rd ed. (American Society of Addiction Medicine, Inc., Chevy Chase, MD, 2003), 395-96.
2. Howard Clinebell, *Understanding and Counseling Persons With Alcohol, Drug and Behavioral Addictions* (Abingdon Press, Nashville, TN, 1998), 426.
3. Allan W. Graham, M.D. and Terry K. Schultz, M.D., eds., *Principles of Addiction Medicine*, 3rd ed., 397.

4. Robert L. Dupont, *The Selfish Brain* (Hazeldon, Center City, MN, 2002), 259.
5. Meyer D. Glantz and Cristine R. Hartel, eds., *Drug Abuse, Origins and Interventions* (American Psychological Associates, Washington D.C., 1999), 125.
6. Melody Beattie, *Codependent No More* (Hazelden, Center City, MN, 1992), 57.
7. "Al-Anon Speaks Out" (Al-Anon Family Group Headquarters, Inc., Virginia Beach, VA., 1981), 1.
8. Neal A. Maxwell, *All These Things Shall Give Thee Experience* (Deseret Book Co., Salt Lake City, Utah, 1979), 37.
9. Boyd K. Packer, "The Candle of the Lord" (Seminar for New Mission Presidents, June 25, 1982).

CHAPTER EIGHT

1. Meyer D. Glantz and Christine R. Hartel, eds., *Drug Abuse, Origins and Interventions* (American Psychological Associates, Washington D.C., 1999), 287.
2. Ibid., 290.
3. Ibid., 291.
4. *Drug Abuse Resistance Education*, "About D.A.R.E", Retrieved October 15, 2003 from www.dare.com/InsideDAREAmerica/Story.
5. National Institute on Drug Abuse, "Risk and Protective Factors in Drug Prevention," Retrieved November 9, 2003 from www.nida.nih.gov/NIDA-Notes
6. Robert L. Dupont, *The Selfish Brain* (Hazelden, Center City, MN, 2002), 276-79.

Appendix A
Suggested Readings

Alcoholics Anonymous, 3rd. Ed. (The Big Book). Alcoholics Anonymous World Services, Inc., New York City, NY, 1994.

Beattie, Melody. *Codependent No More*. Hazelden, Central City, MN, 1992.

Clinebell, Howard. *Understanding and Counseling Persons With Alcohol, Drug and Behavioral Addictions*. Abindon Press, Nashville, TN., 1998.

This book was written for religious counselors. It is comprehensive and easy-reading.

Colvin, Rod. *Prescription Drug Addiction, The Hidden Epidemic*. Addicus Books, Omaha NE, 2002.

Dupont, Robert L. *The Selfish Brain*. Hazelden, Center City, MN, 2002.

Emmett, David and Graeme Nice. *Understanding Drugs*. Kingsley Publishers, London, PA, 1999.

Gorski, Terence T. *Understanding the Twelve Steps*. Simon and Schuster, New York City, NY, 1994.

Harrison, Colleen C. *He Did Deliver Me From Bondage*. Windhaven Publishing and Productions, Pleasant Grove, UT, 2002.

Hidden Treasures Institute, compiler. *Hold On to Hope*. Cedar Fort Inc., Springville, UT, 1996.

Ketcham, Katherine and William F. Asbury. *Beyond the Influence, Understanding and Defeating Alcoholism.* Bantam Books, New York City, NY, 2000.

Levine, Jerome David. *Primer for Treating Substance Abusers.* Jason Aronson, Inc., Northvale, NJ, 1999.

S., Phil. *The Perfect Brightness of Hope.* Massai Publishing, Provo, UT, 2002.

Twelve Steps and Twelve Traditions. Alcoholics Anonymous World Services, Inc., New York City, NY, 1994.

Appendix B

The following organizations offer materials on addiction, treatment and recovery, including general information, books, articles, video tapes and training materials:

American Society of Addiction Medicine (ASAM)
    4601 North Park Avenue, Suite 101
    Chevy Chase, Md 20815
    (301) 656-3920
    www.asam.org

Betty Ford Center
    39000 Bob Hope Drive
    Rancho Mirage, CA 92270
    (619) 773-4100; (800) 854-9211
    www.bettyfordcenter.org

Center for Substance Abuse Prevention (CSAP)
    Substance Abuse and Mental Health
    Services Administration
    5600 Fishers Lane, Rockwall II
    Rockville, MD 20857
    (301) 443-0373

Coalition on Alcohol and Drug Dependent
    Women and Their Children)
    c/o National Council on Alcoholism
    and Drug Dependence (NCADD)
    1010 Vermont Ave NW, Suite 710
    Washington, DC 20005
    (202) 737-8122
    www.ncaa.org

Drug-Addiction.com
    13223 Ventura Boulevard, Suite E
    Studio City, CA 91604
    (866) 762-3712
    www.drug-addiction.com

Hazelden Information and
    Educational Services
    15251 Pleasant Valley Road
    Box 176
    Center City, MN 55012-0176
    (800) 328-9000
    www.hazelden.org

Mothers Against Drunk Driving (MADD)
    511 East John Carpenter Freeway
    Suite 700
    Irving, TX 75062-8187
    (214) 744-6233
    www.madd.org

www.samhsa.gov

National Alliance for the Mentally Ill (NAMI)
    (800) 950-NAMI
    www.nami.org

National Association for Children ofAlcoholics (NACoA)
11426 Rockville Pike, Suite 100
Rockville, MD 20852
(801) 468-0985
www.health.org/nacoa

National Association of Alcoholism and
Drug Abuse Counselors (NAADAC)
1911 North Fort Meyer Drive, Suite 900
Arlington, VA 22209
(800) 548-0497
www.naadac.org

National Clearinghouse for Alcohol
and Other Drug Information (NCADI)
P.O. Box 2345
Rockville, MD 20852-2345
(800) 729-6686; (301) 468-2600
www.health.org

National Council on Alcoholism and Drug Dependence
(NCADD)
12 West 21st Street, 8th Floor
New York, NY 10010
(202) 206-6770
   or
1511 K Street NW, Suite 926
Washington, DC 20005
(202) 737-8122;
(800) NCA-CALL (622-2255)

National Families in Action
    2957 Clairmont Road, Suite 150
    Atlanta, GA 30329
    (404) 248-9676
    www.nationalfamilies.org

National Organization on Fetal Alcohol Syndrome
    216 G Street NE
    Washington, DC 20002
    (202) 785-4585
    www.nofas.org

Merlin O. Baker is a graduate of Brigham Young University. After graduation he served in the Counter Intelligence Corp of the United States Army. He received his Juris Doctorate degree from the University of Chicago Law School and was elected to the Editorial Board of the University of Chicago Law Review.

He practiced law with the law firms of Sidley & Austin in Chicago, Illinois and Ray, Quinney & Nebeker in Salt Lake City, Utah. He served as Chairman of the Board of Visitors of Brigham Young University J. Reuben Clark Law School.

He served as mission president of the Canada-Halifax Mission. He and his wife, Marian, are the parents of seven children. They currently serve as missionaries in the LDS Family Services Addiction Recovery Program and are the mission coordinators for the Salt Lake District. He is also the author of the book, *Charity, Key to Gospel Motivation*.

To visit the author's website, go to

www.understandingaddictionlds.com

0 26575 77778 9